Gilbert Guide® to
Senior Housing

Gilbert Guide® with Nikki Jong

A member of Pen

D0814035

For Gram, and in loving memory of Yin Yin.

ALPHA BOOKS

Published by the Penguin Group

Penguin Group (USA) Inc., 375 Hudson Street, New York, New York 10014, USA

Penguin Group (Canada), 90 Eglinton Avenue East, Suite 700, Toronto, Ontario M4P 2Y3, Canada (a division of Pearson Penguin Canada Inc.)

Penguin Books Ltd., 80 Strand, London WC2R 0RL, England

Penguin Ireland, 25 St. Stephen's Green, Dublin 2, Ireland (a division of Penguin Books Ltd.)

Penguin Group (Australia), 250 Camberwell Road, Camberwell, Victoria 3124, Australia (a division of Pearson Australia Group Pty. Ltd.)

Penguin Books India Pvt. Ltd., 11 Community Centre, Panchsheel Park, New Delhi—110 017, India

Penguin Group (NZ), 67 Apollo Drive, Rosedale, North Shore, Auckland 1311, New Zealand (a division of Pearson New Zealand Ltd.)

Penguin Books (South Africa) (Pty.) Ltd., 24 Sturdee Avenue, Rosebank, Johannesburg 2196, South Africa

Penguin Books Ltd., Registered Offices: 80 Strand, London WC2R 0RL, England

International Standard Book Number: 978-159257-836-8
Library of Congress Catalog Card Number: 2009926593

11   10   09   8   7   6   5   4   3   2   1

Interpretation of the printing code: The rightmost number of the first series of numbers is the year of the book's printing; the rightmost number of the second series of numbers is the number of the book's printing. For example, a printing code of 09-1 shows that the first printing occurred in 2009.

Printed in the United States of America

Note: This publication contains the opinions and ideas of its authors. It is intended to provide helpful and informative material on the subject matter covered. It is sold with the understanding that the authors and publisher are not engaged in rendering professional services in the book. If the reader requires personal assistance or advice, a competent professional should be consulted.

Most Alpha books are available at special quantity discounts for bulk purchases for sales promotions, premiums, fund-raising, or educational use. Special books, or book excerpts, can also be created to fit specific needs.

For details, write: Special Markets, Alpha Books, 375 Hudson Street, New York, NY 10014.

Contents

Introduction

By 2030, when the youngest boomers will turn 65, the U.S. Census has projected that nearly one in five U.S. residents will be 65 and older. And the 65+ age group is additionally expected to increase to 88.5 million by 2050. That's right: over the next 40 years, the number of people 65 and older is expected to double, and the number of people 85 and older is expected to triple!

There has never been a greater number of Americans 65 and older (38.7 million in 2008). As this number increases, so does the number of senior housing options that are emerging to meet their needs. Seniors today can choose from a wider-than-ever-before range of housing options that offer care and support while catering to diverse lifestyles.

As the oldest baby boomers grow close to approaching the traditional retirement age of 65, senior housing builders and developers have responded in force. In 2008 there were a stunning 45,000+ senior housing units under construction in the 100 largest metro areas alone.

While the senior housing industry has experienced a tremendous growth spurt in response to the burgeoning demand, the landscape is changing in other ways as well.

Amid this boom of construction, there is also a strong push to revamp the image of senior housing to make it more attractive to the influx of baby boomers who are in the process of helping their parents choose senior housing, and in the meantime, checking it out for themselves at a later date.

Marketing properties toward active, younger seniors is a strong and growing trend. In 2008, independent living units composed 67 percent of all senior housing units under construction in the largest 100 metros, while the remaining 34 percent comprised nursing home and assisted living units combined. Another emerging trend is expanded options attached to different forms of senior housing, from extended (and ever-expanding) service plans to concierge services at high-end communities, down to the physical type and locale of housing: condo, apartment, cottage, single-family home, high-rise, urban, and suburban.

What does all of this mean for people who are looking for senior housing now? Well, along with all of these options comes the opportunity to pick and choose what you want. But how do you know what you want? And how do you sort through the marketing hype to get to the real scoop?

You can find a tremendous amount of great information about all of the senior housing options both on the web and offline. However, one thing you must be wary of is information that comes directly from independent living, assisted living, or continuing care retirement communities. Clearly, self-reported information has a marketing bias. And that can be a real problem when it comes not only to accuracy, but also to full disclosure about important issues. In the senior housing industry, there are so many referral services, and oftentimes the information about individual residences is either undisclosed or disguised in such a way that it's next to impossible to tell that it came from the residence itself. Taking this information at face value can lead to disastrous results.

In addition, tax laws and senior housing regulations are constantly changing. You need to know where to go for all of this information, and it would be nice if it were all in one place. Unfortunately, that place doesn't exist.

The senior housing industry is booming, and the pool of potential applicants to senior housing is growing by the day. With such an enormous market, which also coincides with the associated health care and supportive services industries, it is no wonder there's an information overload. All of these senior housing residences, especially the brand-new ones, have apartments, rooms, and beds to fill. All of those residences, along with every ancillary service agency they work with, are competing for your time, attention, and your money. Frankly, it's a lot to take in. So if you're confused about what your senior housing options are, we don't blame you.

What you really need to make the most informed choice about senior housing is unbiased information on all of the various options, as well as resources to turn to for more information. And that is what you will find in *Gilbert Guide to Senior Housing*. You don't need to read this book from cover to cover, but we certainly encourage you to do so if you are unsure of what your needs are. Each chapter on the various senior housing options provides an overview of what to expect in terms of services, financial obligations, and atmosphere, as well as more detailed information on what to look for—and what to look out for—in each of these options as you delve deeper into your search.

When we founded Gilbert Guide in 2004, we came from vastly different industries and backgrounds. We certainly were not experts in senior housing and long-term care. But we surrounded ourselves with people who were, and our company quickly became a haven for consumers of these services who, like you, were searching for the best options for themselves or a loved one. Since then, we've learned a lot—particularly because we learned the ropes as consumers first, and advocates second.

For this book, we reviewed hundreds of websites and dozens of books, reports, and articles; and logged countless hours talking to residents and staff members of senior housing, and various aging experts at the ombudsman office, area agencies on aging, and elsewhere. So please allow us to share what we have learned with you as you embark on your journey for finding senior housing.

Perhaps the late Carnegie Mellon professor Randy Pausch said it best in his now-famous *The Last Lecture*: "It's not how long you live, but rather how well you live."

We wish you the best in your search. Let us know how it goes!

Gilbert Guide
215 Second Street, Third Floor
San Francisco, CA 94105
www.GilbertGuide.com

Acknowledgments

We would like to thank the American Seniors Housing Association (ASHA) and National Investment Center for the Seniors Housing and Care Industry (NIC) for their support as we researched this book, and for their generosity in sharing information on the latest senior housing developments, trends, and statistics.

In addition, we would like to thank Kay Paggi, Duane Lipham, Margit Novack, and Carolyn Rosenblatt for their sage advice, dedication to serving seniors and their families, and contributions that have informed this book.

Chapter 1

Considering a Change of Residence

Considering a move to senior housing may be prompted by any number of things. Many seniors in this situation live alone and find that there is just "too much house" to keep up on their own, or find that they could really use some help with everyday activities such as grocery shopping, doing the laundry, and cooking three meals a day. Sometimes getting around is a concern—either because they have begun to have difficulty driving at night and worry that they might not be able to drive soon, or because they don't drive at all. Navigating a house with stairs becomes difficult for seniors with limited mobility. Some seniors who live alone feel lonely or isolated as friends and family members move away and the neighborhood slowly changes. Others develop personal care needs or health needs and require regular assistance or medical care. All of these things are signals that perhaps it is time for a change.

Whatever your personal motivations for considering this change in residence, and for whatever reasons you find your current situation lacking, know that there are many enticing reasons to move into senior housing as well.

This book has two primary goals. The first is to help you understand your personal motivations in a context that poses two simple questions: What do you need? And what do you want? The second goal is to help you find the senior housing option that best fulfills your needs and desires.

The motivations for considering a move to senior housing are as wide-ranging and variable as the individuals taking it under consideration. Health, mental, emotional, functional, and financial status varies from one person to the next. Every person will have unique considerations. And that is the beauty in knowing there is no longer a "one-size-fits-all" mentality regarding aging adults and senior housing. There is, however, one thing that each search process should have in common: a move to senior housing should improve your quality of life. It's that simple.

There are many factors to bear in mind in considering a move to senior housing. This chapter will introduce some of the practical considerations that you should think about as you weigh your options.

Evaluating Your Current Living Situation

Let's start with the basics. First of all, it's important to think about how your environment suits you. This is one of the basic considerations in choosing any type of senior housing arrangement, and it is appropriate and necessary, to think about that now. First ask yourself why you are considering a move.

Perhaps your home has become too much work to maintain, or you have personal or health care needs that would best be served in a supportive residential environment. If you live alone, perhaps you miss the social opportunities of interacting with others on a regular basis. Whatever your reasons are, make sure you identify them clearly.

Are you prepared for a move to senior housing? Is it the most sensible option? If not, are there alternative arrangements you can seek out that would meet your most pressing needs without requiring you to move?

Also consider these questions:

- Is your neighborhood safe?

- Can you get around on your own?

- If you drive, what would you do if driving were no longer possible?

- Is public transportation safe and easily accessible from where you live?

- Are you able to run routine errands like going to the grocery store and drugstore? If so, can you carry your purchases and put them away at home without difficulty?

- Do you have any family living nearby? If not, are there any neighbors or friends you can count on?

With all of these issues in mind, consider how practical it is for you to continue living in your home. What about five or ten years from now?

Thinking About Your Needs, Abilities, and Desires

Most senior housing arrangements offer support services. The type and scope of these services vary by the type of senior housing. But one of the first steps you can take in helping to determine which type of housing would best meet your needs is thinking about your needs, abilities, and desires. Be clear in your own mind about what you expect from a move to senior housing.

What kinds of things do you need help with, or anticipate that you will need help with in the future? What kinds of things can you still do yourself? Here is a list of questions to get you started. It is not a comprehensive list of the services offered by senior housing, nor are all these services offered by each type of housing arrangement. It is simply meant as a jumping-off point to get you thinking.

- Are you able to prepare all of your own meals?

- If you have special dietary requirements, are you able to shop for appropriate food choices? Can you prepare meals with those considerations?

- Can you do the grocery shopping, clean your home, and use the stairs without difficulty?

- Can you walk or get around without assistance?

- Can you do the laundry?

- Do you need help getting in and out of bed or the shower or bath?

- Do you need help getting dressed?

- Are you continent?

- Do you always remember to take your medication, take it on time, and refill your prescription?

- Do you need someone to administer your medication to you (e.g., insulin shots)?

- Are you lonely if you live at home by yourself? Would you like to live in an environment that offers more social opportunities?

If you require or would like help with any of these tasks, or if the social aspect of living among peers appeals to you, then senior housing might be a good option. But you still might be able to stay at home if that is something that you want to do. A professional assessment can help you determine your needs with greater specificity as you continue to examine these issues. See Chapter 11 for more information on getting an assessment.

Every type of senior housing arrangement has advantages and disadvantages, depending on what your needs and desires are. The goal is to find not only the type, but the specific residence that most closely aligns with this personal profile. More than anything, choosing senior housing is a matchmaking process—and the most important component in making a lasting and successful match is compatibility, on as many levels as possible. Remember the two most important questions: What do you need? And what do you want?

For example, safety features are a necessity. In addition to structural safety features, a good senior housing residence should offer security features such as a 24-hour secured facility or security personnel, and a visitor announcement system. It should also be close to emergency medical care (how close is the nearest hospital?). Access to local public transportation is another key consideration. These are things that you may need.

Don't forget about what you want. If you moved to a smaller residence and had housekeeping help, would you spend less time worrying about tidying up before visitors came over? If you lived in a residence in a safe neighborhood with walking paths, would you be inclined to take walks more frequently? If there were a bridge club or weekly worship services, would you be enticed to join? What other kinds of things are important to you?

Sometimes the answers to these questions about what you need and what you want will overlap or coincide; perhaps you need and also want a senior housing arrangement that is safe, affordable, and suits your health needs. Great!

Carefully considering these types of individual issues will help you make a sound decision about the senior housing arrangement and specific residence that will best suit you. The subsequent chapters in this book present those options in greater detail.

Considering Whether a Move Is the Right Choice

If you live at home and are contemplating a move to senior housing, one of the first considerations is whether a move from your current residence is necessary. If your needs could be met at home, would you prefer to stay there?

If so, there may be certain things that you can do to help you stay at home and remain independent. Many seniors who are entering a period of transition may find that while a move to senior housing will be necessary at some point, they're not quite ready to make the move just yet. Help in the form of a housekeeper who comes by to clean once a week or someone you call to maintain the lawn or shovel snow from the driveway as needed might be sufficient enough for you to manage the rest on your own.

If your needs are more evolved but you are still fairly independent, then outside services such as adult day care or adult day health care can provide a social outlet while ensuring that your needs are met. Or if you are still independent and don't require any personal care or health care, then attending your local senior center might be something that interests you.

There are all types of services that can help you stay at home safely, depending on your needs and what is available in your community. Some examples include meal delivery programs and senior companionship services (daily phone check-ins or in-person visits). Certain supportive services such as in-home caregivers can be brought in to ease your daily life in the interim, but for a more realistic longer-term solution, you may need to consider making home modifications that make your physical environment suitable for you.

Home modification measures include any type of major or minor household repairs that could make it easier or possible for you to remain at home safely. But there are also easy fixes you can do to make your home more senior-friendly. Here are some examples of both types of home modifications:

- Install or make sure all smoke alarms are working.

- Wear a MedicAlert pendant or bracelet if you live alone.

- Put a phone in most rooms so that you don't rush to answer the phone if you only have one. Use phones with large buttons that amplify sound. Consider getting a cordless phone that you can carry with you.

- Install handrails near the toilet and in the shower. Get a shower stool if you need it. Use nonskid bath rugs.

- Make sure commonly used items are within reach in all rooms. Avoid standing on a chair to reach items. Use a step stool only if absolutely necessary. If you need help, ask for it. Get a reacher, reach-extender, or grabber device so you can access out-of-the-way items. You can find these in most well-stocked drugstores, hardware stores, and online at www.amazon.com.

- Use night-lights in the bathroom, bedroom, and path in between the two so you can see where you're going at night.

- Use mobility aids such as a cane or walker if you can walk but need a little assistance when someone isn't there to help you.

- Install railings on stairwells, or install stair lifts as necessary.

- Move to the ground floor of your home.

- Replace low-lying furniture like couches, chairs, and beds that are hard for you to get out of once you sit or lie down.

- Get an adjustable bed if you have trouble getting in and out of bed.

- Make sure loose appliance cords are tucked away to prevent tripping and falling.

- De-clutter the house, especially small items on the floor such as doorstops and bathroom scales.

- Remove throw rugs, which are easy to trip on. Also check for loose carpet.

- Keep a list of emergency numbers in easy access, like on your fridge. If someone else makes this list for you, ask the person to list relatives, friends, the fire and police departments, and any other important numbers, such as your doctor's office. Request that the print be large enough so you won't have trouble reading it.

If you have already made a number of these adjustments to your home but are still dealing with challenges, perhaps it is time to seriously consider a move to senior housing. If your neighborhood has changed over the years and it's no longer safe or easy to get around, that, too, is a valid reason for considering a change in residence.

For most people, their home is their most valuable asset. Selling your home and using the proceeds to pay for senior housing and care services is certainly one option.

If you decide to explore this route, what are the steps you would need to take to get your home on the market? This could include minor repairs, such as a leaky faucet or a new paint job, that you have been meaning to make but just haven't gotten around to yet, or it could include major home-improvement projects such as updating rooms that have a certain "retro" flair, gutting the kitchen, replacing worn carpet, installing hardwood floors—any improvements that would make your home more desirable to a buyer.

But perhaps all you can or want to do involves making simple changes that require minimal or no investment other than your time, such as staging techniques that make your home more attractive to potential buyers. These are important to consider, too. Some easy fixes include storing some of your furniture to create the illusion of more space, keeping things clean and "show-ready," rearranging small items for a more appealing aesthetic, and getting a fresh coat of paint on the walls to brighten a room.

If you own your home, there are other ways you can use your equity to pay for senior housing. For more information on financial planning, see Chapter 10.

Identifying Obstacles to Daily Living

What kinds of things do you do every day or nearly every day? Stop and think for just a minute about the activities that fill your day: grocery shopping, driving to see a friend, going to worship services, seeing your doctor, or doing your laundry, for instance. Now think about the factors that impact those things.

Is your home more than one level? Do you have to carry your laundry or groceries up or down the stairs? At some point the steps may be too hard for you to navigate. It is prudent to plan for the possibility even if you have no trouble now.

Do you live in an area of extreme weather conditions? Do you live in an area where you get snow or ice on your driveway? Freezing temperatures, incessant rain, blistering temperatures, sweltering summers, snow piled up high in the driveway—all of these conditions can make it difficult for you to remain comfortably and/or safely at home.

If you can drive now, great. But that won't always be the case. Think about the practicality of living in your home when you can't drive. How will you get around to do the things you need to do?

Do you live far away from family members, or is there someone you could call to come over if you needed help?

Weighing Quality-of-Life Issues

The basic necessities in choosing a senior housing residence are a roof over your head, and personal care or health care as needed. Really, it's pretty simple if you think about it in those terms.

But that would be forgetting the second question in the equation we introduced earlier: what do you want?

Senior housing is a wonderful option for many seniors. When it's a good fit, the senior housing arrangement provides much more than these basic necessities. It also takes into account quality-of-life considerations. Some of these include the following:

- Agility/mobility
- Energy
- Overall health
- Mental health
- Physical health
- Emotional health
- Social opportunities
- Privacy
- Finances/financial freedom
- Independence

Quality-of-life issues are different for each person, and will be prioritized differently. No matter what your personal health care needs and quality-of-life considerations are, and no matter what kind of senior housing arrangement you choose, it is your home. You should feel at home and, within reason, be able to continue to do the things you would normally do in your own home. That includes having visitors over when you want, getting up and going to bed when you choose, making your own decisions about the foods you eat and when you want to eat, and so on. Obviously, every living arrangement will have its own rules, but your rights are protected by laws and regulations. Make sure you consider quality of life in contemplating a move to senior housing.

Making the Decision

Sometimes a move to a particular type of senior housing is dictated by medical necessity, such as a health condition or event that pretty much guarantees you must move into a nursing home. However, in most circumstances, it rarely wraps up into a neat little package that makes it easy to decide what your best option is.

This is a simple but effective tool: write a pros and cons list of every senior housing option that applies to you. Use the following chapters as a basic guide, but dig deep and get personal. Imagine living at each option. How would you feel living there? Pay close attention to your emotional response (listen to your gut; it's telling you something).

Now it's time for the next steps: considering finances, discussing your thoughts with people whose counsel you trust, such as your spouse and family, and taking a deeper look at each senior housing option.

Taking Stock of Your Finances

Considering a move to senior housing requires an assessment of your financial resources. Essentially, you need to answer the following questions: What are the total funds you can count on each month? What are your current monthly expenses? What would your expenses be if you moved? Draw up a basic monthly budget. How much is left over?

Start by identifying all of your personal resources that could be drawn on to pay for senior housing and associated costs. This may include any of the following: income, savings, long-term care insurance, Medicare, Medicaid, Social Security, SSI, other insurance (cash value), annuities, pension (IRA, 401K, etc.), and CDs.

How much do you receive in retirement or pension income, investment income, alimony, or other income? If you decide to sell your current home, what are the tax implications?

List your monthly expenses: mortgage or rent, utilities, food, transportation, medications, incidentals, insurance premiums, entertainment, credit card payments, loan payments, home maintenance, and any other expenses.

Your total income minus your total expenses equals your disposable income. You can use your disposable income to help pay for services, such as care services or home maintenance, to help you stay at home. If you do not have very much disposable income, consider whether you would be willing to sell any of your assets to finance a move to senior housing. If you decide to go this route, how long would proceeds from that asset be able to pay for your needs?

Do you plan on leaving an inheritance? Think about how you want to protect your assets for the future. If you plan to qualify for Medicaid assistance, then you need to start planning immediately. There are people who can help you with this. See Chapter 10 for more information on Medicaid planning and developing a Medicaid/Asset Protection Plan with a professional Medicaid planner.

It's okay if you don't have answers to all of these questions now. But it is important to ask them so you start to develop a clearer picture of what this move might require, and the senior housing options that are viable will also become clearer. See Chapter 10 for more information.

Discussing the Decision with Spouse and Family

Although making a move to senior housing is primarily your decision, it's an important one that can be very difficult to make alone. It's prudent to get other opinions and perspectives when making such a weighty decision. Also more than likely, yours is not the only life that will be impacted by the choice you make. How is this decision likely to affect your spouse? What about your family? If they will be affected by your decision, they deserve to be involved. If you welcome opinions but don't want the decision to be made for you, say so. Repeat yourself if necessary until you are heard, and heeded.

Location, for example, is a primary consideration for most people. Are the facilities you are considering convenient for family members to visit you regularly?

Discussing your reasons for considering a move to senior housing with family members can help them understand what your needs and desires are with regard to your living situation, and give them some footing as how to help you move forward in making a decision and finding an arrangement that works for you. Have the discussion as soon as you can so that you both have a chance to acclimate, and to put your heads together and start researching your options.

Exploring Senior Housing Options

The following chapters offer detailed information about the different types of senior housing and the services and amenities that they provide. But before you jump right in, first take into account the following considerations to help you determine what type of senior housing arrangement may best suit your needs.

- **Independence and privacy.** Are you completely independent and able to live on your own without any assistance? Do you want to continue that lifestyle? How do you feel about privacy? Consider how you would feel living in a senior housing environment where you share communal space with other residents. How would you feel about a communal living situation, such as a shared room in assisted living or a nursing home? Would you be okay with caregivers coming and going from your shared room, and potentially your roommate's visitors as well?

- **Services required.** What kind of services do you require, and which ones would you like to have? Some basic examples include housekeeping, linen service, meal plans, and beautician services.

- **Type of care.** What kind of care do you require? In the senior housing and senior care industries, which often overlap, senior care usually falls into one of two categories: personal (custodial) and medical (skilled nursing). This is a primary factor that will help determine which type of senior housing arrangement suits you best. Do you need help bathing, dressing, or using the toilet? Do you have a chronic illness that requires specialized care? Do you have a condition that is considered progressive? Do you require ongoing care, or 24-hour access to medical care?

- **Duration.** Are you looking into short-term or long-term senior housing options? Short-term options include rehabilitation and respite. Rehab is common for people of all ages after injury or illness, and many nursing homes have dedicated short-term rehabilitation wings where these patients live temporarily as they receive services to help them recover; residents live in another area of the facility dedicated to long-term care. Assisted living facilities and nursing homes both offer short-term options. If you are looking for a long-term living situation, more options may be available.

- **Costs.** Familiarize yourself with the cost ranges of the senior housing options you are considering. If you are planning ahead, ballpark figures are okay. When you get closer to making a decision, however, you'll need to understand the specific costs and any associated fees so that you can determine what you can afford.

Now let's take a quick look at the spectrum of senior housing options:

- **Independent living** offers the most privacy for residents, who typically live in their own apartments. This option is what you might traditionally think of as a retirement community. There are usually no services, or only a limited scope of services offered, as residents are able to live independently. Chapters 3 and 4 discuss independent living options.

- **Assisted living** offers relative privacy, depending on the residence you choose. There may be a choice of private apartments or a shared living arrangement. Social opportunities are emphasized with activities. Assisted living provides personal care assistance with daily activities such as grooming, dressing, cooking, and providing medication and transportation. Some assisted living communities offer memory care for residents who have early-stage memory loss. Chapters 4 and 5 discuss assisted living options.

- **Nursing homes** offer the least amount of privacy of all of the senior housing options. That is because rooms are usually shared by at least two residents, and most residents are frail, elderly, have an illness that requires specialized care, or have severe memory impairment, which requires constant care. Therefore, caregivers constantly monitor residents. Nursing homes provide the same care as described above for assisted living, but also offer skilled nursing (medical) care on a 24-hour basis. Many facilities provide late-stage memory care in a specialized wing known as the dementia unit. In addition, nursing homes provide temporary care for recovery after an illness or accident and specialized care that varies by residence but may include ventilator care, renal care, tracheotomy care, and more. Chapters 6 and 7 discuss nursing home options.

- **Continuing care retirement communities (CCRCs)** combine independent living, assisted living, and nursing home care usually in one location (sometimes with the different components located in separate buildings, but at least on the same campus). Residents can enter at the independent level and transition to assisted living or skilled nursing as their needs change. This is definitely a long-term option. In fact, most CCRCs offer lifetime contracts. The amount of privacy directly corresponds to your place of residence within the spectrum. Chapters 8 and 9 discuss continuing care retirement community options.

For more information on where to get information, support, and advice on choosing a senior housing residence, see Chapter 11.

Planning for the Future

Even if you are blessed with good health now, things can change, and levels of functioning often change as we age. Bad backs, trick knees, coordination or balance problems, decreased hearing and vision, and incontinence are all very common. Planning ahead so that you can prevent unnecessary moves in the future is smart. Try to choose an environment that is designed to support you not only now, but also as you age and the potential need for greater support increases.

You aren't required to utilize all of the services that a senior residence offers; you just use the services you need. Every person will have a different plan once he or she moves in. At most residences, this is very customizable. However, you're much better off having the option of those services being available to you at a later date when you need them, rather than having to go through the process of choosing another senior housing residence that meets your needs later on.

When searching for senior housing, seniors with progressive conditions such as rheumatoid arthritis, Parkinson's disease, or Alzheimer's disease would be well advised to pay particular attention to factors that could affect them in the future. For such seniors it is essential to find residences that have been designed to accommodate these special needs, or are otherwise specially equipped to care for them. If mobility is a concern, some things you may want to look for include ramps, elevators, widened doorways, low-pile carpet, and hardwood or linoleum flooring. If memory care is a concern, you may wish to look for residences that offer specialized care or a separate dementia unit. Even if you don't require special care or support now, you may later on.

Planning for the future is obviously full of unknown factors, but you can use known factors and common sense to make an informed decision. Doing so now can help prevent a disruptive move later. Subsequent chapters will outline other things to look for when you visit the residences in person.

Chapter 2

Independent Living Options

Today's senior housing market encompasses myriad options. Seniors who are healthy but no longer want to live in the home in which they've raised their family may find what they are looking for is independent living. This option enables residents to maintain their independence, coming and going as they please from a private residence that requires little to no maintenance. Many independent living communities cater to seniors who seek enriched lifestyles with organized social activities, offering classes in dance, art, ceramics, woodworking, and more. Independent living residents often have access to convenient supportive services designed to promote their independent lifestyles.

What Is Independent Living?

Independent living communities are sometimes referred to as "active adult retirement communities" or "senior housing with services." This is not to be confused with assisted living, where the arrangement includes housing with custodial care services. While there may be a focus on wellness, independent living communities do not offer custodial or medical care.

The key word in independent living is *independent*. You must be able to manage your residence and personal care needs on your own. However, if you develop a need for custodial or medical care, most communities will allow you to bring in outside caregivers. In this case, you would be responsible for coordinating the arrangement. Independent living communities may have restrictions on the extent of outside care that residents receive while on premises. For example, some communities may not allow residents to use long-term home health care; this is to preserve the independent nature of the community and its residents. If you develop serious health issues that require ongoing care, you may have to move from independent living.

Independent living communities are not licensed by government agencies and are not governed by regulations beyond the housing laws under which they qualify as seniors-only housing providers. Residential agreements and conditions are determined by the organization managing the community. So while there may be a resident council, homeowners' association, or management company to whom you may address complaints, there is no independent regulatory body for the industry. Therefore, it is very important that you fully understand the terms of any contract before you sign. Two professionals who can help you with this are an elder law attorney and a senior real estate specialist (SRES), a Realtor who specializes in seniors-only properties. See Appendix C for contact information for the National Academy of Elder Law Attorneys (NAELA) and the Seniors Real Estate Specialists (SRES) Council.

How It Differs from Living in Your Home

Perhaps the most significant difference you will find between living in your present home and in most independent living arrangements is the convenience factor. In addition to the time residents save by not having to maintain their residence, some independent living options offer built-in services and amenities, which give seniors even more time to pursue their interests. Most independent living residents enjoy a collegial atmosphere with numerous social, educational, and cultural opportunities as well as physical activities to choose from—and just as importantly, the time in which to pursue those activities. No matter which option you choose, however, the wonderful thing about independent living is that the living spaces are specifically designed to suit the needs of senior residents.

Good Candidates for Independent Living

Candidates for independent living must be self-sufficient and in good health. This includes being able to communicate with family members or health care professionals to request help if it is needed. Unlike other senior housing options that provide assistive and health care services, independent living offers seniors a lifestyle of convenience and autonomy, and residents are active, participating members of the community at large, not just the senior residence.

Some people choose independent living because they seek the security of an all-senior community and are attracted to the social opportunities that come with living among a community of peers. Others no longer want to maintain their home and prefer moving to a smaller residence that requires less maintenance. And still others find the convenience of the community's services and amenities well-suited to their lifestyle preferences.

Types of Independent Living Arrangements

There are several types of independent living arrangements, and the accommodations, services, and amenities offered can be quite diverse, ranging from seniors-only apartment complexes that offer no services to extensive campuses with a focus on luxury retirement living, complete with a concierge to fulfill special requests that are not on the basic menu of services.

The quality that most arrangements share is an emphasis on community living. No matter what the physical arrangement is, all independent living communities offer communal space. This shared space can range anywhere from a small sitting room to living, dining, and recreational facilities as well as outdoor areas such as a garden, courtyard, or extensive grounds.

The most common types of independent living options are seniors-only apartments, naturally occurring retirement communities (NORCs), planned independent living communities, and subsidized housing.

Aging in Place

"Aging in place" refers to the concept of seniors staying in their own homes rather than moving out when their health needs change. "Home" may be the house you have lived in for years, but it also applies to any environment where you live and want to stay as you age. Certified aging-in-place specialists (CAPS) are professionals who help seniors age in place safely by making the home environment senior-friendly through a combination of design and equipment. This may include simple changes such as using reflective tape to mark hazardous steps or level changes, and increasing lighting to reduce the risk of falls. But aging-in-place initiatives may also include more involved home modifications such as ensuring there is ample maneuvering space and sufficient storage space within reach, and lowering countertops, sinks, and cooking surfaces as necessary. There are many products and technologies on the market that can help seniors age in place by meeting specific needs that cannot be met by home modifications alone. Independent living providers often consult with aging-in-place specialists to ensure that the community and its individual residences are safe and sustainable for residents. For more information on certified aging-in-place specialists, see the listing for the National Association of Home Builders (NAHB) in Appendix C.

Seniors-Only Apartments

A recent study conducted by the American Association of Retired Persons (AARP) found that over 40 percent of seniors moving to apartment complexes prefer age-restricted communities to age-integrated residences. Senior apartment complexes fit this bill nicely, as qualified age-restricted housing where residents must be at least 62. These complexes are either built specifically for housing seniors, or have been remodeled for that purpose. Either way, these residences are senior-friendly, and in most complexes the individual units are equipped with standard safety features like handrails and emergency call buttons.

Senior apartments that are not part of a planned independent living community may or may not offer extra services, and when they do, the offerings may be basic and limited; for example, there may be light housekeeping and a local shuttle service.

Costs of Senior Apartments

Most senior rental properties fall into the mid-range of costs compared to other independent living options. Rents are typically in line with the market rate for comparable, non-age-restricted rentals in the area, or sometimes slightly less. However, there are also subsidized apartments available for low-income seniors, which will be discussed later in this chapter. Luxury rentals for seniors are a relatively new option, but they do exist. No matter what type of rental property you choose, services almost always cost extra—if they are available—and moving in usually requires a refundable security deposit. In addition, you will have to figure in the cost of utilities. Rent may increase annually. In short, senior apartments are just like other rental properties except that they can be legally age-restricted residences.

Pros and Cons of Senior Apartments

There are many advantages to renting an apartment in a seniors-only complex. For one, apartments that have been designed for senior tenants usually have features such as single-level living, low counters, and raised toilets that make daily living easier to age in place as vision, hearing, and mobility change over time. Also renting a senior apartment usually requires only a short-term commitment; a year is probably the longest lease you will be asked to sign, and many apartment complex owners allow a six-month or even a month-to-month contract. But perhaps one of the most compelling reasons for seniors to downsize from a home to an apartment is to enjoy more autonomy and less responsibility. Downsizing saves considerable time, money, and effort—all of which were previously required to maintain the home. Instead, these seniors can spend their precious time and hard-earned money on family, travel, shopping, entertainment, and other pursuits that are important to them.

However, there are potential downsides to renting a senior apartment as well. Communal living, even when you live in your own unit, is subject to rules regarding pets, smoking, noise, use of common areas, laundry facilities, and so on. This can be a significant adjustment for seniors who are used to living in a house with only their own rules to answer to. And while you may be completely independent now, if your health needs change in the future, it's possible that you'll have to move again. Supportive services that can prolong independence and delay a possible move, such as local transportation and light housekeeping, may or may not be available.

Naturally Occurring Retirement Communities (NORCs)

Home ownership among seniors is at an all-time high. According to the U.S. Census Bureau, the home ownership rate among adults 65 and older is 80.1 percent, higher than the national average of 67.8 percent (2008). And consider the fact that most people don't want to leave their homes. In fact, a 2000 study conducted by AARP estimates that an overwhelming majority of American seniors—89 percent—would prefer to age in place, living the remainder of their lives in their own home. And why wouldn't they, as long as they have access to the things they need to remain independent? Moving would mean leaving behind the friends and neighbors they have known for years, and the community where they have made many memories.

A NORC refers to the phenomenon of neighbors aging together in the same community where they have lived for many years. It is a gradual process whereby the community develops organically over time. A NORC may be a single apartment building or a group of mixed residence types on the same street or immediate neighborhood. No matter what the community looks like, however, they all share one common element: longtime residents aging in proximity to one another. It is estimated that there are approximately 2,000 established neighborhood-based NORCs in the United States. (This estimate doesn't take into account the numerous residential communities of senior residents that do not identify their communities as NORCs.)

As you might expect, the culture of each NORC is unique, owing to many varying geographical, social, income, age-related, and myriad other factors. In addition, due to the gradually developing nature of NORCs and given that most (if not all) residents have lived in the community for so long, these enclaves can be quite private, protected, and difficult to join as a new member.

Despite the fact that NORCs typically develop over time as neighborhood residents age, if the idea of a NORC appeals to you, and you rent or own a unit in a building in which the majority of residents are seniors, it is possible to develop a NORC on your own by applying for your building to become age-restricted.

The Fair Housing Act was enacted in 1968 to prevent discrimination in the housing market based on race, color, religion, or national origin. Later, certain exemptions, including the Housing for Older Persons Act (HOPA) of 1995, were created to allow for age-restricted communities. The Fair Housing Act permits two types of age-restricted communities. To be eligible, the community must have either 80 percent of its units occupied by residents 55 or older, or 100 percent of its units occupied by residents 62 or older. Most age-restricted communities qualify under the 55-plus stipulation, which also makes sense for an emerging NORC, which is likely to encompass a wider range of aging neighbors.

There are many reasons for qualifying a community for age-restricted status and for developing a NORC beyond simply creating a community of peers. Most NORC models, for example, charge annual dues to members, establishing a budget that is used to fund basic services for the community and its members. These may include the following:

- Grocery shopping

- Home maintenance

- Local transportation

- Wellness programs

- Social, cultural, and educational events

- Social workers

- Health care professionals

In addition, the organized community can negotiate better group rates for other necessary services such as home modifications or general maintenance and home health care for those who need it.

The management of a NORC will vary by community. Just as each NORC is unique in its location, neighbors, and group services, so is the management of the community. Some NORCs are self-governing, employing a democratic process among all members of the community, where decisions are made according to majority rule. Others have a more structured process, electing a governing board composed of resident community members and/or parties from the community at large, who together make decisions and enforce rules on behalf of the NORC. Still other NORCs may have a formal board of directors whose members include a mix of professionals in the aging services industry, and who work with a staff that helps carry out the day-to-day management of the community.

One of the most well-known NORCs is called Beacon Hill Village, which was founded in Boston in 2001. Created by a group of longtime neighbor- hood residents who decided that they wanted to stay in their own homes rather than move to senior housing, today Beacon Hill Village is used as a model for creating NORCs across the United States and beyond. See Appen- dix C for more information.

Costs of NORCs

Annual dues for NORCs vary greatly, with best estimates ranging from $15 to 1,000+. The disparity is largely due to some communities obtaining bud- getary funding from city and state sources as well as various grants, and the scope of services offered. Dues are usually based on single/couple status, and membership may be subsidized for those who cannot afford to pay the whole amount. In addition, some NORCs have a sliding scale based on income.

Pros and Cons of NORCs

NORCs enable seniors to age in place and remain close to family, friends, and neighbors. Residents have access to the services they need to remain independent and, in doing so, can nourish their ties to the community and avoid the social isolation that sometimes occurs in institutionalized settings. Staying at home and among a longstanding personal support network provides a feeling of safety and comfort, and NORCs have been recognized as a great option for "house-rich, cash-poor" seniors.

While staying at home has many benefits, the one constant is that these seniors still have the major responsibility of home maintenance. In addition, it may not always be safe to age in place in every residence; seniors may become very frail or develop conditions that preclude living safely at home, even with the proper safety precautions. As with any community, the demographics change over time as the most elderly and frail residents move for necessary medical care or pass on, while their residences go back on the market, bringing an influx of new residents. Moving to a NORC may also be tough for a new resident who is likely to feel like an outsider among friends. Location can be a potential drawback as well. Consider whether the neighborhood is safe and whether access to medical care is an issue in the event of an emergency.

Subsidized Housing for Seniors

The U.S. Department of Housing and Urban Development (HUD) offers financial housing assistance to seniors who meet certain age and income requirements. There is a high demand for housing assistance. Although subsidies are available across the country, large metropolitan areas generally have more options than rural areas. Subsidized housing is usually rented at below-market rates, and there are high occupancy rates, which results in long waiting lists that can sometimes run two years or even longer. Waiting lists may be closed if the number of interested parties exceeds the projected availability of units.

Subsidized housing for seniors is also referred to as "elderly housing" by the government programs that administer it. There are two basic types of subsidies to help program participants afford housing. The first is project-based, where the residence is earmarked for a low-income senior population. The second is tenant-based, where the applicant may select where he or she would like to live, with the subsidy being paid to the landlord, and the tenant paying the balance on the rent. There are several programs offered through HUD for which low-income seniors may qualify: Section 202, Section 8, and public housing.

Section 202 Supportive Housing for the Elderly

Section 202 is the only federally funded low-income housing program designed specifically for seniors. To qualify, applicants must be 62 or older and earn less than 50 percent of the area median income. Many Section 202 housing projects provide basic services such as meal delivery, light house-keeping, and transportation.

The average Section 202 resident is a woman in her late 70s with an annual income of about $10,000. The typical Section 202 unit is a senior-friendly one-bedroom apartment with a kitchen and bath, and safety features such as nonskid flooring, grab bars, and ramps, although these factors are somewhat variable.

Finding Section 202 housing complexes is the easy part. You can find a complete list of program participants on the HUD website at www.HUD.gov. The difficulty comes in finding an available unit, as the number of applicants far exceeds the available units; a 2006 AARP study estimated that there were 10 residents for every unit available. Start by calling every housing provider on the Section 202 list and asking whether they have any vacancies. While it's unlikely that you will find a vacancy by doing this, it's not impossible, and it's a good first step. If you can't locate a Section 202 provider with a vacancy over the phone, the next step is to get your name on the waiting lists, which you will have to do in person.

In addition to the Section 202 application, be prepared to submit the following documentation to establish your eligibility:

- Proof of income (e.g., tax returns)
- Medical and pharmacy bills (used to help calculate your rent)

- Contact information for your previous landlords for a tenant reference; or, if you do not have a tenant history, contact information for personal references who can establish your suitability as a tenant

- A statement from your doctor verifying that you are healthy enough to live on your own

Make copies of these documents and create multiple packets so you can leave one at each site where you apply. As you can see, this is a lengthy and involved process. Get help in calling, preparing the documentation, and even driving to the sites if you can. And don't forget to plan as far in advance as possible!

Section 8 Housing Choice Voucher Program

Administered by HUD, the Section 8 Housing Choice Voucher Program provides tenant-based rental assistance to low-income families, seniors, and disabled individuals. Participants choose their own housing in the private market, using the voucher to pay for a portion or, in some cases, all of the rent. The subsidy is paid to the landlord directly, and the resident pays the remaining balance. Selections are not limited to subsidized housing projects, as in Section 202. The owner must agree to rent the unit under Section 8, and the unit must meet minimum health and safety standards.

Public Housing

Public housing is another HUD-administered program that helps low-income families, seniors, and disabled people find affordable housing. Public housing comes in many forms, from single-family homes and townhouses to apartment complexes and many others in between.

Program eligibility for both Section 8 and public housing is based on the applicant's age, gross annual income, family size (if family members will be living in the unit), and U.S. citizenship or eligible immigration status. To be eligible, you must be able to show a positive tenant history, or, if you do not have a tenant history, be able to produce personal references who can establish your suitability as a tenant.

Section 8 and public housing are not limited to senior participants, and seniors do not receive preferential treatment for their age when applying. Support services and senior-friendly units may not be available. Section 202 is the only government-sponsored program for low-income seniors.

Costs of Subsidized Housing

Section 202 housing is kept affordable because rents are based on a resident's adjusted gross income, which is calculated by deducting approved medical expenses. The resident pays 30 percent of the adjusted income for rent and basic utilities, and the government subsidy pays the remaining balance. Residents are responsible for their own phone, TV, and Internet.

The cost of both Section 8 and public housing vary according to where you live. Income limits for both programs are set by HUD and are based on the area's median income. More information is available at www.HUD.gov.

Pros and Cons of Subsidized Housing

Section 202 housing provides seniors with affordable, safe housing where they live among their peers in seniors-only communities. Many units are senior-friendly, and once you have qualified for the program you can move whenever you choose, as long as you can find another available unit, and with regard to the terms of your lease.

One of the biggest drawbacks of subsidized housing is that the demand far exceeds the supply. Not only does it make it difficult to qualify, but it also translates into lengthy wait times once you do qualify. In addition, there has been a steady increase in qualified applicants as well as a decline in the construction of new housing units due to low funding levels. Some applicants may be troubled by the intrusion into their financial matters. And not all of the units are senior-friendly, which means that as your needs change, you may be required to move yet again. Finally, housing assistance programs are not required to provide supportive services, so while individual properties may offer services through affiliated local agencies, you can expect the services that are offered to be very basic.

The Section 8 and public housing programs offer affordable housing to eligible seniors, and with Section 8 you have the flexibility of choosing where you live to some degree. However, as these programs are not designed specifically for seniors, the housing choices may not be appropriate, and the waiting lists are very long, as seniors do not receive special preference. Additionally, the neighborhoods may not be as safe or convenient for seniors.

Planned Independent Living Communities

Now let's turn our attention to planned communities. Sometimes referred to as "active retirement communities" or "active adult communities," planned independent living communities are age-restricted and designed for seniors. Planned communities include many different forms of housing:

- Single-family homes
- Townhouses
- Duplexes
- Condominiums and apartment complexes
- Mobile or manufactured homes
- Clustered housing
- Standard subdivisions

Some planned independent living communities are expansive, while others are more modest. The resident population may range from a hundred to several thousand. Typically, however, most planned communities are quite large compared to other independent living arrangements.

What to Expect

Planned independent living communities offer a solution for seniors looking to simplify their lives. In most planned communities, residents enjoy a lifestyle free from everyday worries and chores such as cooking, cleaning, driving, and home maintenance.

While the services and amenities offered by each independent living community are unique, here are some of the services you can expect:

- Community events and activities
- Daily meals prepared by a chef
- Housekeeping and linen service
- Live-in management and/or 24-hour security
- Local transportation
- Chapel services
- Travel programs
- Concierge service
- Recreational, educational, and cultural outings and events
- Landscaping
- Banking services

Onsite amenities may include the following:

- Units with kitchenettes or full kitchens
- Exercise facilities
- Swimming pool and spa
- Libraries
- Computer facilities
- Barber shops and beauty salons
- Gardens
- Activity rooms or clubhouses
- Golf courses
- Tennis courts
- Walking paths

As you might expect, the larger, more expensive independent living communities tend to have greater offerings when it comes to services and amenities. However, practically every planned independent living residence is equipped with security and standard safety features, and most communities offer meal plans for residents who prefer not to prepare meals on their own. Onsite recreational activities and day trips are standard offerings, and some communities even employ full-time activity directors. Services may or may not be included in your costs; be sure to ask which, if any, will incur an extra charge.

> One way to tell if a service is not included in your basic costs is if it's billed as "optional." Optional just means you'll have to pay for the service if you want it.

Range of Communities

Planned independent living communities are big business. With the graying of America's baby boomers, builders have answered with independent living communities that speak to every special interest. From university-affiliated communities to golf-, beach-, and gourmet food- and wine-oriented communities, there is a place for everyone.

And if none of these options speak to you, don't worry. Although there are an increasing number of these types of niche communities, it represents only a slim margin compared to the more traditional independent living communities, whose shared motto seems to be: "Come one, come all; and if you like it here, stay."

University-based retirement communities are flourishing, growing from about two dozen to over 100 in the last decade. These communities have a focus on continuing education for seniors. The communities are usually located on or nearby the university campus, and classes are offered at a reduced rate or even for free. Stanford, Notre Dame, Duke, and Cornell are among the top universities that have built their own retirement communities or are affiliated with a nearby one.

Buying vs. Renting

Planned independent living communities may offer residents the option of leasing or buying a housing unit. Owning a unit in an independent living community is similar to owning a condo anywhere else. You are not responsible for common areas, but you have full responsibility for the interior of your home (not including plumbing or other physical systems). As an owner, you share the costs of maintaining the exterior grounds and building(s), as well as the salaries of building managers and staff, and insurance—all paid through the Homeowners' Association (HOA).

Buying a unit also enables owners to build equity. Many buyers view the purchase of their housing unit not only as a real estate investment, but also as a potential source of future income, which can help finance unexpected health care costs. If you like the community, are prepared to live there for the foreseeable future, and can afford to buy a unit, buying may be a good option for you. Consult a financial professional who can help you understand all the financial implications of purchasing a housing unit that is part of an independent living community. One of the most important questions to ask is: What are the rules regarding resale?

Renting gives occupants the freedom to enjoy all of the same services and amenities that the community offers to owners, but without the significant upfront financial investment. In addition, if the arrangement doesn't work out, the renter can simply pack up and leave (with regard to the rules stated in the contract). Renting is a great option for seniors who are looking to simplify their lives: you don't have to pay property taxes or make decisions about how to maintain the residence or grounds; if something is broken, you can simply call maintenance to have it fixed. No fuss, no muss. Of course, renting can become quite expensive over time, particularly with periodic rent increases, so sometimes longtime renters end up paying more than owners in the long run.

Costs of Planned Independent Living Communities

Planned communities typically fall on the high end of the cost spectrum for independent living. This is particularly true for communities that require residents to buy the housing unit. Like condominiums, the cost of a purchasing is indexed to the cost of comparable housing in the area. Services are typically included in a monthly fee, which also covers taxes and utilities.

Financing for a condo is the same as it is for buying a single-family home, through a mortgage and monthly payments to the mortgage holder. In addition, there is a monthly HOA fee.

Some planned independent living communities require an entrance fee (also called a "buy-in" fee) in addition to a monthly rent, while others merely require a month-to-month all-inclusive payment. Prices range widely, depending on the size of the unit, the services offered by the community, and the area where it is located. Whether buying or renting, in the long-term, the cost of an independent living facility is generally much less than an assisted living facility or nursing home. When you factor in the basic services that are included at an independent living community, the total cost may be cheaper than maintaining a home.

A financial planner can help you determine how to pay for independent living costs by tallying your current costs of living and estimating what they would be in a retirement community, helping you draft a plan that also accounts for your long-term-care financial needs.

Pros and Cons of Planned Communities

Planned independent living communities offer all the comforts of home but without the hassles of home maintenance or household chores. Planned communities are all about convenience living and enjoying your retirement to the fullest. The services and amenities are designed to not only promote residents' independence, but also to encourage them to pursue their interests and continue to develop and grow as individuals. The expansive nature of many planned independent living communities, in addition to a variety of planned activities, also lends itself to residents forging new friendships with others who have similar interests and passions.

Of course, planned independent living communities can be very expensive. While the social aspect of this option is one of the most attractive features to many, some people might feel restricted by the current resident group, many of whom might not share your interests. Another potential disadvantage for owners is the need for cooperative decision-making within the community's HOA on discretionary spending priorities.

Chapter 3

Choosing an Independent Living Option

Now that you know what your independent living options are, it's time to do some research on options in the area you're interested in. Independent living follows that same golden rule of real estate: location, location, location. Do you want to stay in your neighborhood, your town, your state? Or are you considering a move to be nearer to family or a warmer climate? Once you've made that decision, it's time to start narrowing your choices.

You might start by choosing a general location, but there are many other factors that are important to consider up front. For most of us, cost is usually the next consideration. What can you afford? Chapter 10 will help you determine how you can pay for independent living through a combination of resources so you can answer that very question. And now is the ideal time to book an appointment to speak with a professional financial planner, who can explain your payment options and help you draft a plan that fits your budget and your life.

Appendix C lists the contact information for the Financial Planning Association (FPA), the National Association of Personal Financial Advisors (NAPFA), and the Society of Financial Service Professionals, three excellent organizations through which you can locate a qualified financial planner.

The Physical Visit: What to Look For

No matter what type of independent living arrangement you choose, and no matter how much research you do before choosing, there is nothing that can replace an old-fashioned visit. Your research process is not complete until you make a visit. This is something you must do in person, and it is one of the most important factors in making your choice. Ask someone you trust, such as a family member, to join you on the visit if possible. Having a second set of eyes and ears will be helpful, both for making observations on your visit and discussing your impressions afterward. Your loved one may notice things that you miss or be able to think of additional questions, or simply provide support and a fresh perspective. All of these things are invaluable.

Remember when we mentioned that changing your living situation to suit your lifestyle is all about the convenience factor? Well, part of that convenience includes comfort. We're not talking about "luxury" comfort that involves a personal butler and 1,000-thread-count bed linens, but something more along the lines of feeling comfortable and secure in your new home. There's nothing that can confirm this like visiting your potential new home in person.

Use your five senses while you're there. Examine the neighborhood, property, and living units. Listen to what current residents and staff have to say. If possible, sample the food while you're there. Try out the furnishings in the common areas (and units, if they come furnished) to see whether they're comfortable. And don't forget to stop and smell the roses! That is, if there's a garden. The point is, take advantage of being there in person to make notes that you'd never be able to get from a brochure, through online research, or over the phone.

And here's the number-one thing to look for: are you comfortable? Can you picture yourself living here?

Checklist for Touring Independent Living

Have you ever gone to the grocery store for a meal you're planning, only to return home and realize you're still missing some of the ingredients you need? Well, so have we! That's what this checklist is for. Bring this book with you on your tour so you can make sure that no matter what independent living option you choose, the community meets all of your expectations. As with any recipe, you'll probably find yourself adapting this checklist to suit your preferences, and in the end, we hope, you'll wind up with a result you are proud to share and enjoy with family and friends when they visit.

It may be helpful to think of the following questions in terms of how they meet your needs. For each element that is important to your quality of life, ask yourself whether your findings are acceptable or not acceptable, and whether there is there a compromise that can be reached.

Location

- ☐ Is the community's location convenient to your doctor, family, restaurants, shopping areas, and/or house of worship?
- ☐ Is parking available for you and your guests?
- ☐ Is there access to public transportation?

Safety

- ☐ Does the neighborhood appear safe? Do you like the neighborhood?
- ☐ Are you comfortable with the level of security in the community? Is the front desk staffed 24 hours a day?
- ☐ Is the community prepared for natural disasters? Ask about smoke alarms, fire drills and evacuation plans.
- ☐ Are there grab bars, handrails, and elevators in communal areas?
- ☐ Is the lighting adequate?

Residences

- ☐ How are residences assigned, or can you choose your own?
- ☐ Do the size, view, and location meet your needs?
- ☐ Will your furnishings fit, or are furnishings provided?
- ☐ Does the residence have sufficient storage space? Can you reach the cupboards and top shelves?
- ☐ Is the kitchen equipped with a stove, sink, and refrigerator (i.e., can you cook and store food in your residence)?
- ☐ Are residences equipped with smoke alarms, sprinklers, and a call system?
- ☐ Are there grab bars by the bed and in the bathroom?
- ☐ Are housekeeping services available? How frequently?
- ☐ Are residents allowed to smoke in their units? Are nonsmoking units available?

Staff and Management

- ☐ Do the staff seem friendly and helpful when they interact with residents?
- ☐ Do they introduce you to residents and encourage visiting with them?
- ☐ Do staff members appear to interact positively with each other?
- ☐ Are there staff members you can communicate with if you prefer speaking a language other than English?

Residents

- ☐ Is the age, ethnicity, or faith of your neighbors important to you? That is, do you prefer interacting with people similar to you? If so, take note of the residents you encounter to determine compatibility.
- ☐ Do residents seem about as active as you?
- ☐ Do residents interact positively with one another?
- ☐ Do the residents seem happy?

Care

- ☐ Are you allowed to hire caregivers should you require care?
- ☐ What are the processes for emergency hospitalizations?
- ☐ Is there an on-site pharmacy, or a delivery service for prescriptions and medical supplies should you need them?

Meals

- ☐ Are three daily meals included, or is there a meal plan available for a fee?
- ☐ Are special dietary needs accommodated?
- ☐ Are snacks available in between mealtimes?
- ☐ Is there a communal dining room or restaurant(s)?

☐ Can you have meals delivered to your residence, and if so, is there a fee?

☐ If you are able to sample a meal on your visit, is the food fresh and tasty?

Activities

☐ Are you interested in the scheduled activities?

☐ Are there daily exercise offerings?

☐ Are worship services available?

☐ Is transportation provided for appointments, shopping, activities, and emergencies?

Community Features and Aesthetics

☐ Is the indoor temperature comfortable? What about the noise level?

☐ What amenities are available on site?

☐ Is there adequate access to common areas such as activity rooms and dining areas?

☐ Do the residence and common areas meet with your aesthetic expectations?

Notes

_____

_____

_____

_____

_____

_____

_____

Questions to Ask Before You Sign the Contract or Lease

There are so many things to think about when choosing any new home, and independent living is no exception. The best thing you can do to ensure that you make the right choice is to be prepared, and there is no better way to do that than by researching each option you're interested in, visiting those communities in person, and asking lots of questions. The following is a list of questions to get you started. Incorporate them into your research process. At a minimum, get answers to these questions before you sign the contract or lease:

- Is there a waiting list? How long is it?

- Do the community's services meet your needs?

- If the facility is sponsored by a nonprofit organization (e.g., a church or university) and managed under contract to a commercial firm, what are the conditions of the contract?

- Is there a HOA, resident council, or organization through which residents can voice their views on the management of the community?

- What is the policy on overnight guests?

- Are pets allowed? What is the policy?

- What happens if you decide to move out, or if your health needs dictate that you must move?

- Can the community terminate your housing agreement, and if so, under what conditions?

- Do residents own or rent their units?

- As an owner, do you have the right to sublease your unit?

- What are the policies regarding resale of a unit?

- What are the upfront costs, including deposit, entrance fees, community fees, and any other fees?

- What is covered by a resident's entrance fee (if one is charged)? Is all or a portion refundable, and if so, under what conditions?

- How often are fees increased? What are the criteria for increasing fees?

- How much do you get back if you move out?

- Which services are optional and at what fees?

Chapter 4

Assisted Living Facilities

Assisted living is a relatively young industry that has developed largely over the past two decades. Since then, there has been a tremendous amount of growth, with assisted living providers rapidly expanding to meet the increasing demand for housing with supportive services for seniors who are still mostly independent and don't require around-the-clock access to medical care.

As is often the case with this type of fast-track industry growth, the regulations are still catching up. Unlike nursing homes, assisted living facilities are not regulated on a federal level. They are regulated by the states—and with great variation. In some states, assisted living regulation is still in its infancy. As such, you won't find the same standardization of services or styles of facilities that you will find in more established types of senior housing that have a longer history and are subject to a system of standard regulation. In fact, even the terms used to refer to assisted living residences aren't standardized. There are dozens of designations that states use to refer to various types of housing-with-services arrangements that qualify as assisted living.

According to the Assisted Living Federation of America, the average age of an assisted living resident is 85. As this average age has increased, assisted living facilities have expanded their service offerings and evolved to offer more services to help residents age in place longer and avoid having to move to a nursing home prematurely.

Not surprisingly, assisted living residents spend a great deal more time at the facility than do their peers in independent living. This changes the dynamics, certainly. Perhaps the most significant outcome is that residents end up spending more time together, underscoring the communal aspect of assisted living. Therefore, there is an emphasis on building, sustaining, and participating in the community in most assisted living arrangements.

What Is Assisted Living?

"Assisted living" is a broad term that encompasses a wide range of residential facilities that provide care to seniors. The facilities provide room and board, 24-hour staff supervision, and an array of services. Basic offerings include light housekeeping as well as assistance with personal care activities such as hygiene, dressing, eating, and getting around for those who require help. Transportation for doctors' appointments, shopping, and errands is usually provided or arranged for, and most facilities offer three meals a day in addition to snacks in between meals. Additional services that are commonly offered, sometimes for an additional fee, include laundry and medication management. And keeping in line with the emphasis on community, most assisted living facilities have planned recreational and social activities, scheduled community events, and outings.

Assisted living seeks to extend seniors' independence, enabling them to live as independently as possible for as long as possible. Residents are encouraged to continue making their own decisions about lifestyle and health care in a safe, supportive environment that promotes quality of life. As with independent living (see Chapter 2), the support services offered within assisted living facilities enable residents to spend their time doing the things they enjoy.

Assisted living facilities are licensed and regulated on a state-by-state basis through their state's Department of Health. Each state sets care and safety standards that the facilities must meet. In addition to the license from the health department, the facilities must hold certifications for any specialized services that are provided, such as Alzheimer's and dementia care.

However, it is important to keep in mind that assisted living facilities are *not* considered medical facilities. As such, they are not required to have doctors, nurses, or even certified nursing assistants on staff, although many facilities do have medical staff either on site or on call in case of emergency. Because assisted living facilities are considered nonmedical facilities, staff members cannot administer medication to residents, but they may store and distribute residents' medications, and they may provide verbal reminders to residents to take their medications.

Residents who require nursing or medical care that the facility is unable to provide may be able to hire a private-duty nurse or caregiver. Every assisted living residence will have its own rules, so this may not always be possible.

And if the residents' care needs progressively develop so that the person requires constant (rather than short-term or intermittent) nursing, the resident may need to leave the facility, as outlined in the agreement.

In addition, because assisted living residences are prohibited from providing skilled care, some facilities obtain a hospice waiver, which allows residents who have been certified by their doctor to be eligible for hospice care, to stay and be treated by trained hospice caregivers, rather than enforcing a move during such a trying time. In facilities that have hospice waivers, hospice caregivers are hired privately by the resident or resident's family.

Intake Meeting and Assessment

As you might imagine, there is a wide range of needs in assisted living. Some residents may require very little assistance while others need a lot of help. Prior to moving in, the facility management will meet with applicants to determine how much care they are likely to require upon moving in. This is known as the intake meeting. Part of the process includes an overall assessment. Among other things, assessments typically cover the following:

- Cognitive health
- Physical health and functioning
- Behavioral status
- Communication ability
- Cultural preferences
- Spiritual needs and preferences

Assessing applicants helps the facility ensure that they are adequately staffed and equipped to meet the needs of all residents. The goal of the intake meeting is not just to identify the senior's care needs in a functional assessment, but also to help the management team and applicant become acquainted and guarantee a good fit for both parties.

Levels of Care

Because every resident has unique needs, it is necessary for assisted living facilities to determine set levels of care. Setting levels of care helps the facility to streamline the caregiving process by ensuring that the facility and residents maintain a schedule and that residents' care needs are met in an efficient and cost-conscious manner.

Some assisted living facilities include the costs of care in the monthly rate, but most do not. The most common pricing structure is based on levels of care, although services at some facilities may be offered only on an à la carte basis. Sometimes both pricing structures are utilized. Three or four levels of care is typical, with a higher level of care translating into higher monthly payments. If a combined pricing structure is in place, specialized services (such as incontinence care and medication management) may be charged on an individual basis in addition to costs for the basic levels of care. In case you haven't already guessed, combined pricing structures that incorporate levels of care and offer à la carte services are famously complicated if you are not familiar with them, so make sure you understand what your financial obligations will be before signing an agreement.

Now a bit of good news: although the pricing structures may be complicated, establishing levels of care actually helps facilities to simplify their pricing for costs of care. When a resident requires more care, his costs rise. This avoids the need to reassess costs every time a resident's needs change. Levels of care are also convenient for the residents and their families: with upfront pricing, you know how much you'll be paying every time a change occurs in care needs, and can plan accordingly.

The components of each level of care vary from facility-to-facility. Many facilities use a point system to determine a resident's required level of care. Residents who are determined to be independent after an assessment and who do not require any help will not be charged for care. This may also apply to residents who only need verbal reminders to complete the activities of daily living (ADLs). You will hear about ADLs frequently in senior housing and senior care. They include personal hygiene, grooming, bathing, dressing, toileting, feeding, transferring, and medication management. The components that typically determine the level of care a resident requires include these ADLs, plus mobility, continence, caregivers, eating, and dementia.

Bathing

There are two factors to consider: whether the resident requires assistance in showering or bathing, and if so, how often help is required. For example, a resident who needs help washing her hair once a week but can otherwise manage independently would require a lower level of care than a resident who requires help with all bathing activities.

Dressing

The assessment will measure whether a resident can dress without assistance. Again, there are two factors to consider: whether the resident is physically able to dress on her own, including managing zippers and buttons, and whether she is able to make appropriate clothing choices for the weather or occasion (e.g., not a nightgown for an outing).

Grooming

Grooming includes activities such as washing one's face, brushing hair and teeth, and shaving. At lower levels of care, residents may need reminders or to be supervised by caregivers during grooming activities; at higher levels, residents may require hands-on assistance.

Mobility

How much help does a new resident need to get around? This includes not only walking, but also moving from a seated to a standing position and getting out of bed. At the highest level of care, a resident might need a Hoyer lift to be transferred from a bed, bath, or wheelchair. Residents at lower levels of care may only require minimal assistance with walking or moving to a wheelchair. At move-in, most assisted living facilities require that residents be able to walk into the facility on their own, although most will allow the use of a walker.

Continence

Incontinent residents who are able to manage without assistance will not be charged for incontinence care. Higher levels of care include residents who exhibit behavioral issues around their incontinence, such as becoming combative when an aide attempts to change their adult diapers. Incontinence care may be considered a specialized service at some facilities, with costs determined on a case-by-case basis, rather than incorporated into the basic levels of care.

Caregivers

Residents who require care from multiple caregivers simultaneously are likely to be placed at a higher level of care. A few examples of residents who may fall into this category include those who require a high level of pain management, those who have a tendency to wander or leave the facility, those who are at a very high risk for falls (determined during the assessment), and those who require assistance with physical therapy exercises.

Eating

Eating assistance encompasses all levels of care. At the lowest level, residents may be able to feed themselves but require help cutting their food. Higher levels of care may require the presence of a caregiver at all meals, for residents who are physically unable to eat independently, are at risk of choking, or have issues with consuming or hoarding food items that present a dietary, safety, or medical hazard.

Medication Management

At the lower levels of care, caregivers assist residents in filling prescriptions and supervising or administering oral or inhaled medications. Residents who require help with injectable medications or require nursing supervision are placed at a higher level of care. Advanced medication management for residents who take multiple medications may also require a higher level of care if the number of the resident's medications surpasses the facility's threshold; for example, six or seven medications may bump the resident to a higher level of care even if all of the medications are taken orally.

Dementia

Residents with Alzheimer's or dementia are usually placed at a higher level of care. These residents must be reassessed regularly, as most dementias are progressive. Most facilities determine the needs of a resident with dementia based on the following three criteria:

- **Diagnosis:** When was the resident diagnosed with dementia? How severe is it?

- **Behavior:** Has the resident exhibited combative or inappropriate behaviors? Does he or she wander?

- **Monitoring:** Does the resident require constant monitoring or are a few daily checks sufficient?

Types of Assisted Living Facilities

Assisted living facilities come in all shapes, sizes, and forms, from small private homes licensed to care for a few individuals, to great sprawling campuses that resemble grand estates, which may cater to 100 or more residents. Most assisted living arrangements offer private apartments that range from studios to multiple bedrooms, although many smaller residences offer rooms rather than apartments.

However, there's one thing that most of these assisted living sites have in common: the look and feel of home. If you've never visited an assisted living facility before, and you're a little apprehensive about what to expect, you may be in for a pleasant surprise. The two big things that set assisted living facilities and nursing homes apart is the kind of care that is provided and the environment in which it is provided. Assisted living evolved as an option for seniors who could no longer live at home, but who weren't ready for a nursing home. So by design, it had to be an attractive option. Don't let the clinical-sounding "facility" fool you. While you might find safety features like built-in grab bars and conveniences such as modified kitchens and bathrooms that make access easier, they won't upset the aesthetics, and you certainly won't be sleeping in a hospital bed!

Personal Care Homes

Personal care homes are small-scale assisted living residences, usually with just a few residents. Typically, personal care homes are private homes operated by a small staff. Because the homes and staff are small, the amenities and services may be limited, and the personal care that is available may be offered on a schedule rather than as needed or preferred. So for example, residents may bathe according to a set schedule. Depending on the home, residents may have a choice of a shared or private room and shared or private bathroom. Like other community senior housing arrangements, there are communal spaces as well, typically a dining room and space for socializing and activities. One attractive feature of personal care homes is that they tend to be significantly less expensive than the larger assisted living communities, as overhead costs are generally much lower.

Personal care homes may also be referred to as residential care homes, group homes, adult homes, boarding homes, adult foster care, domiciliary care, or assisted living. This variation is a reflection of the nonstandard regulations in the industry. Even when the offerings are the same, the names of personal care homes may vary by geographic location, licensing requirements (e.g., number of residents), and other factors. Regulations vary by state. In some states, personal care homes may be licensed to offer limited medical care, although it is not common.

Personal care facilities were among the first assisted living residences to develop. Since then, many states have adopted regulations and licensing requirements for these small-scale assisted living residences. However, many homes, particularly those that house and care for only a very few residents, have not complied with recent regulations, and many operate without licenses. If you are considering a personal care facility, be sure to verify licensure with the state licensing office.

The Consumer Consortium for Assisted Living lists the contact information for each state's licensing agency on its website at www.ccal.org. See Appendix B for more information.

You may be wondering why licensing is important if personal care homes do not provide medical care. Regulation is necessary for several reasons. First, state licensing laws hold these care providers to a certain standard of care. When unlicensed (and therefore unregulated) facilities continue to operate, it is the consumer who takes the greatest risk. Not only will the service offerings vary greatly from location to location, but so will the quality of the services and amenities. For these reasons it is necessary to confirm licensure.

Assisted Living Facilities

Assisted living facilities are generally larger-scale residences, providing housing and services for up to several hundred residents in one location. But the size of the facility and grounds as well as the number of residents can vary greatly. According to the Assisted Living Federation of America, most communities have between 25 to 120 units.

With a larger budget, bigger staff, and more residents than personal care homes, assisted living facilities usually offer a greater array of services and flexibility in when those services may be accessed. Indeed, residents of assisted living facilities may enjoy a greater deal of autonomy with services being offered on an as-needed basis rather than on a regimented schedule as is often the case in personal care homes. If a resident would like assistance bathing, for example, it can usually be arranged without disrupting the caregiving schedule or having the resident wait for "her turn."

Like any other type of housing, assisted living facilities run the gamut from budget to luxury. At one end of the spectrum are basic (sometimes shared) accommodations with limited amenities and services, geared toward a low-income resident population. On the other end are high-end facilities with luxuriously appointed apartments where residents have access to every convenience and comfort imaginable. And of course, there are assisted living facilities that offer everything in between.

In addition to group social activities, the more lavish facilities may offer classes, lectures, film screenings, and wellness and exercise programs. Many upscale facilities are located in gated communities, providing an additional element of security. And many offer amenities that rival those of a swanky country club, with rolling lawns, manicured gardens, state-of-the-art fitness centers, swimming pools, spas, and more.

Veterans Homes

Veterans homes provide government-subsidized housing and care to eligible veterans. There are 135 veterans homes currently operating in 49 states (all but Alaska) and Puerto Rico, serving more than 30,000 individuals. The Department of Veterans Affairs (VA) provides three levels of care within its network of veterans homes, including assisted living, skilled nursing, and acute care, all of which are broadly referred to as "community residential care." Assisted living services are sometimes referred to as "domiciliary care." Both short-term rehabilitative care—for applicants whose goal is to return home—and long-term residential care are available. An overwhelming 80 percent of veterans home residents receive some type of skilled nursing care.

Veterans homes have eligibility requirements that are set by the state, so the application process varies depending upon the location of the residence. However, all applicants must meet three basic criteria to be eligible:

- Must be a veteran discharged under honorable conditions

- Must be a resident of the state in which he or she is applying

- Must meet certain financial guidelines as determined by the state

In addition to veterans homes, the VA offers benefits and special pensions to help pay for the cost of assisted living at nonveteran facilities. See Chapter 10 for more information.

Dementia Care Facilities

Many assisted living facilities are able to provide dementia care for residents who require it, and some even have separate dementia units, but until recently, few facilities actually specialized in this type of care, offering it simply as an adjunct to their standard services. Lately there has been a movement toward specialized dementia care facilities, where services and sometimes even the physical environments are tailored to the special needs of residents with dementia. Staff members at these facilities have additional training and experience in dementia care.

Most forms of dementia are progressive, which makes it even more important to choose the right facility from the beginning to avoid having to move again. Moving is hard for most people, and as we get older, it usually becomes even more difficult. Consider this along with the fact that adjusting to new environments can be especially traumatic for people with dementia.

One of the most important considerations in evaluating a dementia care facility is the experience of the staff. The Alzheimer's Association has identified three key areas that care providers must emphasize in order to offer continued quality of life to residents with dementia: food and fluid consumption, pain management, and social engagement. Because dementia hampers communication, staff members must be skilled at recognizing nonverbal signs and cues to ensure that residents are well fed and hydrated, are not in pain, and do not become socially isolated or withdrawn.

In addition to offering the personal care and supportive services found at most assisted living arrangements, dementia care facilities must go beyond meeting these basic needs. The cognitive and behavioral issues that go hand in hand with dementia create unique challenges that specialized care facilities are designed to meet. A few examples of this in the physical environment may include color-coded floors and hallways, visual cues, suitable lighting, and heightened security. Other considerations include offering suitable small group or one-on-one activities that promote each resident's skills and interests, maintaining secure walking areas, and taking additional safety pre-cautions for wanderers. (Wandering tendencies are common in people with dementia, and can be dangerous if a resident wanders away from the facility and becomes disoriented.) Dementia care facilities are locked residences, which means that residents cannot leave on their own, enabling the staff to keep a close watch on them. It also means that there is no open access to the facility, so all visitors and staff must be identified before entering.

Costs of Assisted Living

There are many factors that affect the cost of assisted living. Some of these include the size and type (i.e., room or apartment, private or shared) of the accommodations, the amenities offered by the facility, the resident's level of care, and additional services that are utilized. Location is also a major factor; as a general rule, urban areas cost more than suburban or rural areas. The two primary costs no matter where you decide upon are rent, also known as the "base rate," and cost of care. As you may recall, some facilities include the cost of care in the base rate, although most do not.

Fees are due monthly. Most residents and families pay from personal resources or through a long-term care insurance policy, although there are subsidies available for veterans and Medicaid-eligible seniors. See Chapter 10 for a detailed explanation.

Monthly costs for assisted living may range from $400 to 5,000+, depend-ing on the location, accommodations, services, and amenities. This cost represents the base rate, which typically includes room and board and meals. The MetLife Market Survey of Nursing Home and Assisted Living Costs, published in October 2008, found that the national average monthly cost of a private assisted living apartment or private room with private bath was $3,031. The data is based on information from 1,518 assisted living facilities, including personal care homes, and does not reflect costs of care. The same study found the national average base rate for dementia care to be $4,267 per month.

Additional services and utilities are usually charged separately, and there may be a fee to be put on the waiting list if one exists. Deposits may be required for pets and smoking, if applicable, and move-in (usually the equivalent of first and last month's rent). Wait-list fees and deposits may or may not be refundable.

Pros and Cons of Assisted Living

Just as in independent living, residents can leave chores such as cooking, housekeeping, and maintenance to someone else, freeing up time for more enjoyable pursuits. One of the primary goals of assisted living is to sustain residents' quality of life in as many ways as possible. This applies to the quality of care as much as it does to the aesthetics of the community and its residences—it should feel homey!—and the principle of enabling residents to continue making their own choices. Your living space is your own, and you will be able to decorate it as you please (in accordance with the facility's rules). In most circumstances, you can bring your own furnishings from home if you like. Many facilities welcome residents with pets. The environment is safe, with 24-hour supervision and oftentimes a locked facility. With individualized care plans tailored to each resident's unique needs, residents and their loved ones can rest assured that their daily needs will be attended to.

One of the most positive qualities of assisted living is undoubtedly the social aspect that is promoted through active participation in the community and taking part in the activities that are offered. Many assisted living residents and their families have recognized the importance of ongoing social engagement. Assisted living can be a wonderful choice for isolated seniors and those who have outlived spouses and friends, as well as seniors who haven't skipped a beat, but are simply ready to move to a more supportive environment.

While assisted living emphasizes residents' independence as much as possible, there is considerably less privacy and autonomy than you would have if you continued to live at home where you are on your own schedule. In any type of community living, even when you have a private apartment, your independence will not be as great as it was before. Activities and meals are usually offered on a schedule, which means that you may have less flexibility in your choices.

Perhaps the biggest drawback is cost. Assisted living is notoriously expensive, and the costs only get higher as care needs increase. And let's not forget one very significant consideration: with all but a small handful of assisted living facilities, you will not be guaranteed on-site medical care in the event of an emergency as you would with a nursing home.

Chapter 5

Choosing an Assisted Living Facility

Assisted living offers both housing and custodial care, filling a much-needed gap in the senior housing market, but the erratic regulation makes choosing the right assisted living facility that much more complicated than choosing the right independent living arrangement, because your decision is twofold. Not only do you have to select the best housing environment for your needs, but you must also ensure that the facility you select is properly licensed and meets the regulations set by the state, and consider the supportive services and care that you will require, both now and in the future.

One of the trickiest parts of the whole process is anticipating what those needs might be in order to prevent moving again unnecessarily. Under the right circumstances, you may never have to move again. While your health and many other factors may affect this outcome, the point is that you want to choose a place where you can live for a long time, a place that will meet your current needs and continue to be able to provide support and care as your health needs change over time.

Cost and care are usually the first factors that people consider in choosing an assisted living facility, and necessarily so. Proximity to loved ones is another primary consideration. But don't forget that *you* will be the person living there, day in and day out, not your loved ones. So don't choose a facility simply because it's the most affordable option, or the one that's most convenient for friends and family to visit. Ideally, the facility you choose will be a good match on both counts. But ultimately, you should choose the facility where you feel you will have the best quality of life. Visiting in person to get a feel for what it's really like there will help you make this determination.

The Physical Visit: What to Look For

You'll be looking for a lot of things when you visit the assisted living facilities that are on your shortlist, which the checklists and questions in this chapter will help you with. Many of those things, such as whether the facility is properly licensed, will be easy to check off your list because they are purely objective measures. But other measures, which are equally important, are much more subjective.

Take independent living and nursing homes, for example. In both of these senior housing options, there is a slimmer margin of difference in the needs of each resident population. Independent living residents require very little, if any, support, while nursing home residents tend to be frail and require a lot of care. In assisted living it's different; the range of needs is much broader. You're likely to notice a lot of variance in the needs and functional abilities of residents when you visit the facilities on your list. You may notice that the residents at one assisted living facility are younger and more active, while the opposite is true at another. It's also common to find a mix of residents under the same roof. And keep in mind that these dynamics change over time.

At some point you may have heard about "facility culture." This is very important to observe when you visit. The attitudes, values, and goals of residents and staff, and how the two groups interact with each other, are the building blocks of facility culture, and together they should paint a picture of what everyday life is like at the facility—and what your life would be like there if you were to move in.

Checklist for Touring Assisted Living

While there are perhaps more varied factors to consider in choosing an assisted living facility, the basic approach to choosing is very similar: make a shortlist of favorites, visit those facilities in person, and ask lots of questions before, during, and after your visit. Following is a list of questions that you can use to get started. Add your own questions to the list and bring all of them with you on your visit. You may not get answers to all of these questions during your visit, but make sure you get answers to the questions that matter to you—*all* of them—before you sign any contract with the facility.

Location

- ☐ Is the location of the facility convenient to your doctor, family, restaurants, shopping areas, and/or house of worship?

- ☐ Is parking available for you and your guests?

- ☐ Is there access to public transportation?

Safety

- ☐ Does the neighborhood appear safe? Do you like the neighborhood?

- ☐ Are you comfortable with the level of security in the facility? Is the front desk staffed 24 hours a day?

- ☐ If there is a separate dementia unit, is it locked? Are there door alarms and WanderGuard in place? (WanderGuard encompasses a host of technologies, from alarm systems to door monitors and wearable monitoring devices, which help prevent or curb dangerous wandering behaviors.)

- ☐ Is the facility prepared for natural disasters? Ask about smoke alarms, fire drills and evacuation plans.

- ☐ Are there grab bars, handrails, and elevators in communal areas?

- ☐ Is the lighting adequate?

Apartments or Rooms

- ☐ How are rooms or apartments assigned, or can you choose your own?

- ☐ Does the size and location meet your needs?

- ☐ Will your furnishings fit, or are furnishings provided?

- ☐ Is there sufficient storage space? Can you reach the cupboards and top shelves?

- ☐ Is the kitchen equipped with a stove, sink, and refrigerator (i.e., can you cook and store food in your residence)?

- ☐ Are all rooms or apartments equipped with smoke alarms, sprinklers, and a call system?

☐ Are there grab bars by the bed and in the bathroom?

☐ How clean are the bathrooms (if you would be sharing with another resident)?

☐ Can the bathrooms accommodate wheelchairs or walkers?

☐ Are housekeeping services available? How frequently?

☐ Are residents allowed to smoke in their units? Are nonsmoking units available?

Staff and Management

☐ Does the staff seem friendly and helpful when they interact with residents?

☐ Do they introduce you to residents and encourage visiting with them?

☐ Do staff members appear to interact positively with each other?

☐ Are there staff members you can communicate with if you prefer speaking a language other than English?

☐ Is there a doctor or nurse on staff or on call?

☐ Are staff members available to provide 24-hour assistance with custodial care?

☐ Is the availability of care on nights, weekends, and holidays the same as it is on weekdays?

Residents

☐ Is the age, ethnicity, or faith of your neighbors important to you? That is, do you prefer interacting with people similar to you? If so, take note of the residents you encounter to determine compatibility.

☐ Do residents seem about as active as you?

☐ Do residents interact positively with one another?

☐ Do the residents seem happy?

Care

- ☐ Are you allowed to hire outside caregivers if you require skilled care that the facility cannot provide? Will the facility help you secure these services?

- ☐ What is the plan in the event of a medical emergency or hospitalization?

- ☐ Is there an on-site pharmacy, or will the facility arrange delivery service for prescriptions and necessary supplies (e.g., incontinence supplies)?

- ☐ How often are residents assessed?

- ☐ Is there a written service plan or care plan for each resident?

- ☐ What kind of medication assistance is provided?

- ☐ What are your options if you develop dementia after becoming a resident?

- ☐ Under what circumstances would the facility no longer be able to house and care for a resident? How is this determined?

- ☐ Does the facility have a hospice care contract?

Meals

- ☐ Are three daily meals included?

- ☐ Are special dietary needs accommodated? Is there a dietitian or nutritionist on staff?

- ☐ Are snacks available in between mealtimes?

- ☐ Is there a communal dining room or restaurant(s)?

- ☐ Can you have meals delivered to your apartment or room, and if so, is there a fee?

- ☐ If you are able to sample a meal on your visit, is the food fresh and tasty?

Activities

- ☐ Are you interested in the scheduled activities?
- ☐ Is daily exercise offered?
- ☐ Are worship services available?
- ☐ Is transportation provided for appointments, shopping, activities, and emergencies?

Facility Features and Aesthetics

- ☐ Is the indoor temperature comfortable? What about the noise level?
- ☐ Are there any unappealing odors?
- ☐ What amenities are available on site? (Examples include a beauty shop, activities room, fitness equipment, computer access, and outdoor gardens or patio.)
- ☐ Is there adequate access to common areas such as activity rooms and dining areas?
- ☐ Are the apartments or rooms and common areas appealing?
- ☐ Do the hallways and common areas accommodate wheelchairs and walkers? What about the residences?

Policies

- ☐ Is there a waiting list? How long is it?
- ☐ If the facility is sponsored by a nonprofit organization (e.g., a church or university) and managed under contract to a commercial firm, what are the conditions of the contract?
- ☐ Is there a resident or family council or other organization through which residents can voice their views on the management of the community?
- ☐ What is the policy on overnight guests?
- ☐ Are pets allowed? What is the policy?

☐ What happens if you decide to move out, or if your health needs dictate that you must move?

☐ Can the facility terminate your housing agreement, and if so, under what conditions?

☐ What is the policy on medication administration?

☐ What is the refund policy?

☐ What is the move-out policy?

Costs

☐ What are the upfront costs, including deposits and any other fees? Which of these are refundable and under what conditions?

☐ How often are fees increased? What are the criteria for increasing fees?

☐ How much do you get back if you move out?

☐ Which services are included in the monthly costs? Get a printed menu of services with costs.

Notes

_____

_____

_____

_____

_____

_____

_____

_____

_____

Before You Sign the Contract

Assisted living facilities often refer to the contracts they use with their residents as a "Resident Agreement." For all intents and purposes, the document functions both as a lease and an agreement that the resident will abide by the facility's rules and policies. It should outline the terms that facility and resident both agree to, but sometimes not all of the rules and policies will be included. If they aren't, ask that they be included, or, at the very least, ask for a copy of the facility's rules and policies so that you know what you are implicitly agreeing to by signing the contract. The resident agreement should also disclose the facility's services, including costs and additional charges as well as admission and discharge criteria.

Choosing the assisted living facility that is right for you requires lots of planning and due diligence. We hope that once you have made this decision, it is the right one. But if it ends up not meeting your expectations, here's one thing that's nice to know: many assisted living facilities do not require a long-term financial commitment up front, which means that new residents who don't like the facility can leave without being penalized. Make sure you understand what your rights are in this regard before signing the contract. And if at first you don't succeed in finding the right assisted living facility, take heart and try again. Armed with the right information, you will succeed.

In addition to the touring checklist, be sure to take these important steps:

- ☐ Ask to see the facility's license and verify the facility's licensure status with your state department of health.

- ☐ Obtain a copy of the contract and review it with an attorney and/or financial advisor who is familiar with this type of contract and who can explain the terms to you. You can find an elder law attorney who specializes in this area through the National Academy of Elder Law Attorneys at www.naela.org.

- ☐ Ensure that all promises made verbally are stated explicitly in the contract.

- ☐ Read the facility's state inspection report. Not all states require that assisted living facilities be inspected, so this may not be available where you live.

☐ Check with the Better Business Bureau (www.bbb.org) and the long-term care ombudsman in your state to determine whether any complaints have been filed against the facility. If you find complaints, follow up with facility management to ask how they have been resolved. Call 202-332-2275 or visit www.ltcombudsman.org to find your local ombudsman.

☐ Ask for a copy of the facility's disclosure statement. The disclosure statement is a document issued by the state, which details all of the facility's services and policies in a uniform manner, making it easier for you to compare facilities. Not all states require assisted living facilities to use disclosure statements, so this may not be available in your state.

☐ Ask for a written description of the procedures for filing a complaint or grievance.

Chapter 6

Nursing Homes

Nursing homes are what many people still think of as the only housing option for seniors who are no longer able to live at home on their own. While this may have once been the case, it's certainly no longer true. The burgeoning independent and assisted living industries prove that there are plenty of options for today's seniors. As these industries have developed, expanded, and refined their services, they have settled into their place on the spectrum of senior housing. The further down the spectrum, the closer the tie is between housing and care. That's where today's nursing homes fit in, providing both housing and on-site access to medical care, and offering residents an array of services to address their physical, medical, and social needs.

The Culture Change Movement

The "culture change" movement, a progression toward resident-centered care, is one of the more recent developments in the nursing home industry. The dual foundational principles of culture change are establishing a homey environment that is capable of meeting the medical and health needs of residents, and re-establishing residents' autonomy as much as possible. Now more than ever, nursing homes are striving to help residents continue to lead meaningful lives in a comfortable, secure environment, and in a way that honors their dignity.

Historically, nursing homes have been structured, clinical environments in which meals, activities, and routine care were offered on a schedule that suited the caregivers and other nursing home staff. Resident-centered care has shifted this paradigm in two key ways: first, by adopting a new philosophy of care that embraces quality of life, and second, creating an environment that is conducive to putting this philosophy into practice. In other words, culture change supports a physical design that is homey and warm, not sterile-feeling and hospital-like.

Nursing homes that are part of the culture change movement and have adopted a philosophy of resident-centered care have adapted their environments in any number of ways, from creating larger common areas for residents by relocating and rebuilding nursing stations in a more discreet fashion, to installing partitions in shared rooms for a greater degree of privacy. Some facilities have smaller buildings, separate from the main nursing home, that resemble a family home and function independently as a household. The management in these "homes" may even be run independently from the main facility, developing their own house rules and procedures. This can also occur in small units within the nursing home itself. Through daily interaction in a more intimate environment, sharing meals and participating in activities together, the idea is that this encourages close relationships between residents and caregivers and nurtures a strong community.

Culture change doesn't necessarily require extensive remodeling or construction, however. There are many ways in which the principles of culture change can be adopted. Giving residents more choice and autonomy in their daily lives and routines is another key indicator of culture change, whether that means extending access to breakfast even if it's "past" the scheduled meal time, or allowing residents' beloved pets to live in the nursing home with them. Other examples include offering more private rooms (vs. shared), and encouraging residents to bring their own furnishings from home when they move in, creating comfortable, familiar surroundings.

Jennifer Mikula, the nursing home administrator of Palm Gardens in Ocala, Florida, sees resident-centered culture change as a shift from a medical model to a social model, which calls for treating residents as people first, and as patients when necessary. Indeed, the facility's philosophy of care is to focus on wellness rather than illness.

Culture change and resident-centered care have far broader implications beyond improving residents' daily lives. Facilities that have implemented culture change measures have seen clear clinical improvements in residents, including increased mobility, desirable weight gain, and improved mood and cognition. Not only that, staff satisfaction and staff retention are significantly on the rise at the same facilities, proving that implementing culture change and resident-centered care initiatives makes nursing homes a better place to live and work.

Two extremely successful examples of culture change in nursing homes are the Eden Alternative and The Green House Project. Both program models have been replicated at nursing homes across the country. More information and resources on culture change in nursing homes are available through the American Health Quality Association at www.ahqa.org. See Appendix C for listings and contact information on all three of these organizations.

What Is a Nursing Home?

Nursing homes are residential facilities that provide skilled nursing care. Also known as skilled nursing facilities or convalescent homes, nursing homes may market themselves as extended care or long-term care facilities, but regardless of the name they go by, the licensing is the same.

In addition to skilled nursing care and custodial care, nursing homes offer a wide array of services, which are determined by state regulation, so they vary depending upon where you live. At most nursing homes you can expect the following basic services:

- A furnished room, private or shared

- Three nutritious meals a day, with snacks in between mealtimes

- 24-hour access to skilled nursing care, with care provided under a doctor's supervision

- Custodial care, including incontinence care

- Medication management

- Social and recreational activities

- A comprehensive resident assessment, including an individualized, written care plan

- Housekeeping and linen service

- Basic transportation (e.g., to doctor's appointments)

In addition to the basic services listed above, other common services and specialized care that may be available for an additional fee include the following:

- Rehabilitation: physical, occupational, speech, and respiratory therapies

- Pharmacy, lab, and radiology services

- Optometry services

- Podiatry services

- Dental care

- Hospice care for terminal illness

- Specialized care for Alzheimer's disease and dementia, renal conditions, and Parkinson's disease

- Transportation

- Laundry service

- Beauty/grooming services (e.g., haircuts and styling, and nail care)

If you're planning a move to a nursing home from your family home or an independent or assisted living residence, you should be prepared for several major differences. For one, the living space is much smaller. Shared rooms—known as "semi-private" rooms—are the norm, although private rooms are available at some facilities. Another major difference is that residents of nursing homes tend to be much frailer than their assisted living counterparts. As they require around-the-clock access to medical care, be prepared for a much more sedentary population. And while a number of nursing homes, following the principles of culture change, have vamped up their décor in recent years, many other nursing homes still exude an institutional feeling.

According to the latest data (2007) from the U.S. Census Bureau, 68 percent of nursing home residents were women. The median age of all residents was 83.

Intake Meeting and Assessment

When new residents are admitted to a nursing home, they undergo a comprehensive health assessment. Some states require that the assessment be completed in as few as 7 days, but in general it must be completed within 14 days of the resident's admission date. Quarterly reviews help determine whether a reassessment is necessary. At a minimum, residents should be reassessed annually, and more frequently if health needs require it.

A comprehensive assessment involves more than simply gathering health information. The assessment is likely to inquire about your habits, preferences, routines, and relationships as well as your general outlook on life. The information from the health assessment is used to draft your personal care plan.

A care plan is an individualized plan of care that is tailored to each resident. You, and your family if you wish, are encouraged to be proactive in drafting your care plan with the staff, communicating your desires, questions, and concerns during the process. Your involvement ensures that you will receive the care you need while your preferences are respected. Care plans are dynamic documents that are adjusted as necessary. This is what a typical care plan might address:

- The nursing, medical, and custodial care services you require and how often you require them

- Types of medical equipment or supplies you need, such as a wheelchair, walker, or incontinence supplies

- Any dietary restrictions you have (e.g., diabetic, renal, low-salt), as well as food preferences and sensitivities

- Your personal heath goals, such as whether you want to improve your health in general, become more independent, or even improve sufficiently enough so that you can be discharged, and how the care plan will help you achieve those goals

- Which staff members will perform the specific care tasks that you require?

Levels of Care

Nursing homes are a unique senior housing option because they accommodate residents with a very wide range of needs. On one hand, there are residents moving from their family homes or from living with relatives or from assisted living facilities, all with increasing needs that require skilled nursing care. Others have recently been discharged from a hospital for surgery, acute illness, or another condition from which they are recovering, and for which they need short-term skilled nursing. Nursing homes are at a certain crossroads in this way. Because of the wide-ranging care that nursing homes provide, the levels of care are usually grouped into short-term and long-term care.

Some nursing homes specialize in a certain type of care as well. If you are being discharged from the hospital, the hospital discharge planner or social worker can help you find local nursing homes that fit your needs. Within the levels of care, nursing homes may also distinguish between "light," "medium," and "heavy" care, which is then addressed in each resident's individual care plan.

Long-Term Care

Most residents who require long-term care live the remainder of their lives in the nursing home. These residents tend to be in relatively poor health. The long-term care residents of nursing homes are elderly, frail, and many have chronic conditions that require constant monitoring or treatment such as injections or ventilation. Or if they are bedbound, they will require constant supervision to ensure they're getting enough food and fluids and to prevent bedsores and infections from occurring. Progressive conditions such as Alzheimer's disease and Parkinson's disease are common in long-term skilled nursing residents.

Short-Term Care

Short-term care is perhaps better described as "temporary care," as it can last anywhere from a few days to a few months. It all depends on the patient's condition and recovery, which is unique in every situation.

Two of the most common types of short-term nursing care include rehabilitative and respite care. Nursing homes can be a great short-term option for rehabilitative care, as an intermediate stop between hospital and home. Short-term nursing home stays are often used in conjunction with another senior housing option, where the senior will return to after making a recovery. Many short-term residents have recently been discharged from the hospital and require rehabilitative care. Recovering from an illness, a fall, or a stroke are all common reasons for a short-term nursing home stay.

Respite care, which provides temporary relief to the seniors' usual caregivers, is another common type of short-term care. Nursing homes may have a requirement of a minimum amount of days for a short-term respite stay.

Hospice care is also known as "comfort care" by providers because it eases the pain of the dying and those with terminal illness. The patient's doctor and the hospice medical director must certify that the patient is terminally ill, with a life expectancy of six months or less, in order for the patient to be eligible for hospice care.

Hospice care is administered by trained hospice caregivers, not nursing home staff. Because nursing homes are not legally required to contract with hospice providers, hospice care is not available at every nursing facility. Find out whether there is a hospice contract in place at every nursing home you are considering. To read more about hospice care in nursing homes, visit www.medicareadvocacy. org. The Center for Medicare Advocacy offers a wealth of information about Medicare-related topics, including the insightful article "Hospice in the Nursing Home."

Activities

Activities are a very important part of maintaining residents' well-being and helping them feel at home. Not only do activities provide stimulation and fun, they keep residents involved in the nursing home community and help build trust and relationships. Activities promote residents' physical and cognitive health by encouraging them to engage their senses in interesting ways.

Participating in activities also helps to break up residents' days and stave off the boredom and social isolation that are widely associated with nursing homes. Participation isn't limited to residents, either; group activities often involve staff, family, and visitors as well. A good nursing home should offer a variety of one-on-one or group activities, or a combination of the two, that appeals to a diverse range of abilities and interests. They should also be inclusive, even if not everyone is able to participate. Sometimes simply observing others take part in an activity can have a positive effect.

And don't think we're talking just about playing Bingo here. Sure, it's still a popular pastime in a lot of facilities, but today, many nursing homes are offering activities like foot massages, manicures, and other in-house spa treatments; Monday night football gatherings; lunch outings; gentle exercise sessions; and yes—even cocktail hours.

Checking Service History

Unlike assisted living, the nursing home industry is highly regulated. Nursing homes are licensed medical facilities that are regulated by the state departments of health. In order to participate in the federal assistance programs Medicare and Medicaid, nursing homes are required to meet more than 150 regulatory standards set by Congress to protect residents. These standards address an extensive set of topics ranging from the care the residents receive, to the setting in which it is provided, to the training of the caregivers who provide it. Nursing homes are inspected every 12 to 15 months by a team of trained, professional inspectors that includes at least one registered nurse. Facilities that are found to be underperforming and are required to take corrective measures are inspected more frequently. The results of the inspection are public and are available on Medicare's website at www.medicare.gov.

If there's one thing you take away from this chapter, let it be this: *review the facility's most recent inspection report before making your decision.* This is an easy and necessary step! You will find more detailed information on checking the service history of nursing homes in Chapter 7.

Residents' Rights

Nursing home residents have certain rights and protections that are established under state and federal law. Nursing homes are required to furnish a copy of these basic rights to each new resident. These rights vary by state, but according to Medicare, they usually include the following:

- **Respect.** You have the right to be treated with dignity and respect.

- **Services and fees.** You must be informed in writing about services and fees before you enter the nursing home.

- **Money.** You have the right to manage your own money or to choose someone else you trust to do this for you.

- **Privacy.** You have the right to privacy, and to keep and use your personal belongings and property as long as it doesn't interfere with the rights, health, or safety of others.

- **Medical care.** You have the right to be informed about your medical condition, medications, and to see your own doctor. You also have the right to refuse medications and treatments.

In addition to the basic rights listed above, federal law dictates that all nursing homes must abide by and promote the following rights for their residents:

- **Freedom from discrimination.** Nursing homes must comply with Civil Rights laws, which prohibit them from discrimination based on race, color, national origin, disability, age, or religion.

- **Respect.** You have the right to choose your own schedule, including when you go to bed and get up in the morning, and which activities you choose to attend and participate in.

- **Freedom from abuse and neglect.** You have the right to be free from verbal, sexual, physical, and mental abuse, corporal punishment and involuntary seclusion. Nursing homes are required to investigate all complaints and suspicious injuries within five working days of the incident.

- **Freedom from restraints.** It is unlawful for nursing homes to use physical or chemical restraints unless it is medically necessary. You have the right to refuse restraints, which will be honored unless you pose a risk of harm to yourself or others.

- **Information on services and fees.** Nursing homes must inform you, in writing, about all facility services and fees before you move in, and you must be informed when services or fees change.

- **Money.** In addition to your basic right of choosing who will manage your money, detailed previously, you may ask the nursing home to manage your finances. If you choose that option, the nursing home must allow you access to your money, place it in an interest-accruing account, protect your funds from loss, and, in the event that you die, return the funds to the person handling your estate, with a final accounting and within 30 days.

- **Privacy, property, and living arrangements.** You have the right to privacy, including having private telephone conversations. Nursing homes are not allowed to open your mail without your permission. You have the right to use your personal belongings as long as they don't interfere with the rights, health, or safety of others. Nursing homes are required to protect your property from theft. You have the right to share a room with your spouse and to reject a move to an inappropriate room. You must be notified prior to a room change or change in roommate.

- **Medical care.** Federal law establishes extensive rights for nursing home residents regarding medical care. These include your right to be informed about your health status, including medical condition(s) and medication(s). You have the right to see your own doctor, to self-administer medications (unless the nursing home finds this unsafe), and to refuse medications and treatments. You also have the right to access all of your records and reports within 24 hours. In addition, the nursing home is required to notify your doctor, your legal representative (if known), and your family when (1) you are involved in an accident that results in an injury or may require a doctor's intervention; (2) a deterioration occurs in your health, mental or psychosocial status in a life-threatening condition, or there are clinical complications; (3) your treatment needs to change significantly; or (4) when the nursing home decides to transfer or discharge you from the home.

- **Visitors.** You have the right to spend private time with visitors and to refuse visitors. Nursing homes must permit your family to see you at any time, as long as you want to see them.

- **Social services.** Nursing homes must provide you with or help arrange the social services that you require. They must also provide appropriate activities for you.

- **Leaving the nursing home.** You have the right to leave or move out of the nursing home at any point you choose. However, many nursing homes have policies that require advance notice for moving out and are usually subject to a fee if ignored. Additionally, certain health insurance policies require you to be at the nursing home continuously to avoid an interruption in coverage.

- **Complaints.** You have the right to make a complaint without fear of punishment. Nursing homes are required to take prompt action.

- **Protection against unfair transfer or discharge.** You can't be sent to another nursing home, or forced to leave your current nursing home except under the following conditions: if it is necessary to protect your welfare, health, or safety, or the welfare, health, and safety of others; if your health has declined so that the nursing home is no longer able to meet your care needs; if your health has improved and you no longer require skilled nursing care; if you are not able to pay for the services you have received; or if the nursing home closes. Except in emergencies, nursing homes are required to give you a 30-day written notice of their plan and reason to discharge or transfer you.

- **Family and friends.** Family members and legal guardians may meet with the families of other residents and may establish and participate in family councils. With your permission, family members can help in drafting your care plan. If a family member is your legal guardian, he or she has the right to review your medical records and make decisions on your behalf.

- **Resident groups.** You have the right to form and participate in a resident council to discuss issues and concerns about the nursing home's policies and operations. The nursing home is required to supply a meeting space and must listen and respond to the grievances and recommendations of the group.

Many nursing home applicants are concerned about smoking. Some nursing homes are nonsmoking facilities, meaning that smoking is not allowed on the premises. If a nursing home is not a designated nonsmoking facility, then it must allow residents to smoke if they choose. To prohibit them from smoking would violate their residents' rights. However, nursing homes may restrict the areas in which smoking is allowed; in some facilities, only outdoor smoking is accepted, and in others, smoking may also be allowed in designated indoor areas. Resident rooms are typically nonsmoking. If you have a medical condition that is aggravated by smoke, or if it simply bothers you, you can request a nonsmoking roommate. This is a wise choice even if the room is nonsmoking, since lingering tobacco smoke can still be bothersome.

Cost of Nursing Homes

It should come as no surprise that nursing homes are very expensive. According to the October 2008 Metlife Market Survey of Nursing Home and Assisted Living Costs, the national average for a semi-private room in a nursing home was $191 per day in 2008, while the average daily rate for a private room was $212. Also in 2008, the highest daily statewide average for a private room was $577 and $566 for a semi-private room, both in Alaska. The lowest daily statewide averages were in Louisiana, which averaged $127 per day for a private room, and Minnesota and Oklahoma, both of which averaged $121 per day for a semi-private room. For information on how to pay for nursing home care, see Chapter 10.

Pros and Cons of Nursing Homes

With the growing culture change movement, nursing homes are emerging as a more appealing senior housing option than ever before. Undoubtedly the biggest benefit that nursing homes offer is around-the-clock access to skilled nursing care administered by trained, professional staff in a safe and secure environment. In combination with nutritious meals and snacks, engaging activities, and individualized care plans, nursing homes offer specialized solutions tailored to each resident. And extensive industry-wide regulations ensure greater consistency, a baseline of quality care, regular inspections, and punitive measures for facilities that do not measure up. For residents and their families, this alone can provide significant peace of mind.

Nursing homes also have their disadvantages. Although residents have a right to privacy, for example, the concept of privacy becomes more subjective when your personal space is limited. Most long-term nursing home residents are in relatively poor health and have very little independence while living in the facility, as they are very dependent upon the staff for care and supportive services. Nursing home costs are incredibly high, so most people who enter a facility paying out of pocket eventually end up spending their resources until they become eligible for Medicaid, the federal assistance program for low-income seniors. You can find more information about Medicaid in Chapter 10.

Chapter 7

Choosing a Nursing Home

Moving is never easy, no matter where the destination. But out of all the senior housing options, nursing homes can seem like the biggest jump to make, whether you're moving from your family home, independent living, or assisted living. Even if you know that moving to a nursing home is the right choice for your circumstances, coming to terms with this decision can be difficult. That is why it's so important to make sure you're choosing the right facility for you. This chapter will equip you with the information you need to make an informed choice.

Many people have been through this before you, so don't be daunted by the process. Here's some good news: finding the right nursing home is actually much more straightforward than finding the right assisted living facility. There are several reasons for this. For one, there are far fewer nursing homes to choose from, which narrows your search considerably. Another factor that narrows the field is the method by which you will pay. Be it out of your own pocket, through a long-term care insurance policy, or through Medicaid, your payment method will determine which facilities make your shortlist, as not all facilities accept all forms of payment—and many have limited space available unless you will be paying out of pocket. When you do begin to tackle that list, thanks to strict state and federal regulations, the inspection data on nursing homes is reliable, current, informative, and in-depth, making it much easier to measure the performance of individual nursing homes. And finally, your visits to the facilities themselves are likely to make or break your decision. From visiting in person, you will be able to glean a lot of information—from evidence of culture change and resident-centered care to whether you like the environment and the current residents, and so much more.

Believe it or not, there are just three basic steps to choosing a nursing home. First, you must develop a list of facilities to consider. Second, compare those options. And third, visit the facilities that have made their way to the top of your list. If it sounds simple enough, that's because it is. Finding the right nursing home just takes time. And it is well worth the time and effort to get it right.

To draft an initial list of nursing homes, you may first want turn to people you already know and trust, such as your doctor, clergy, social worker, family, friends, and neighbors. You may be surprised at how many of them have had experience with a loved one in a nursing home. Ask for their advice and recommendations on local facilities to consider. Again, as with assisted living, you may choose to develop this list based on geographical considerations—such whether the facility is close enough so that family and friends can visit often.

Nursing Home Compare

After you've talked to the people around you and have gotten their recommendations, a great place to continue your search is Nursing Home Compare (see Appendix B). An online application on the Medicare website, Nursing Home Compare helps you find and compare nursing homes that are certified to participate in Medicare or Medicaid. You can search for the factors that are most important to you, such as location, type of ownership (e.g., for-profit or nonprofit), number of beds, whether the facilities have a resident and/or family council, and much more. Nursing Home Compare offers detailed information on the most recent health inspections, staffing data, quality measures, and fire safety inspections.

The next step is comparing the nursing homes on your list, and this is where it begins to get tricky. The most important factor is the quality of the care provided by the nursing home. While a nursing home may be close to family and fit your budget, it defeats the purpose if the facility you choose provides substandard care. Perhaps you are wondering why a substandard facility wouldn't be shut down by regulators if it were really that bad. The short answer is this: regulations are a double-edged sword; on one hand, they make choosing a nursing home easier for individuals and families like yours because you can see the areas in which the facilities measure up (or don't) to quality standards during an inspection. But on the other hand, because nursing homes are given ample opportunity to make up for their mistakes, this "opportunity" can also mean that you end up choosing a substandard facility during the interim period after a failed inspection.

Nursing home care is very expensive, and most people cannot afford to pay out of pocket for an extended period. In fact, 7 out of 10 nursing home residents are on Medicaid. So while nursing homes are not required to be certified by Medicare or Medicaid, most facilities choose to undergo certification because doing so enables them to accept and care for a greater pool of residents.

Understanding Nursing Home Inspection Results

The Centers for Medicare & Medicaid Services (CMS; see Appendix C) is run by the federal Department of Health and Human Services.

Nursing homes are licensed by state governments, which contract with CMS to ensure that nursing homes that participate in the Medicare and Medicaid programs meet eligibility requirements. This is done through onsite inspections.

Inspections occur about once a year unless a nursing home performs poorly, in which case state inspectors may schedule subsequent inspections to follow up and make sure corrective measures have been taken. The point of regular inspections is to investigate the nursing home's standards of daily operating procedures, safety, and care. In order to obtain an accurate assessment, inspections are unannounced. In fact, it is illegal for an inspector to advise or warn a nursing home about an upcoming inspection.

During an inspection, the team of inspectors observes and investigates the facility's care processes, interaction between residents and staff, overall environment, and fire safety. They talk to residents, family members, direct caregivers, and administrative staff in addition to reviewing residents' clinical medical records. All of these factors help inspectors determine whether the nursing homes meet minimum quality and performance standards.

As noted in Chapter 6, there are more than 150 regulatory standards, set by Congress, which have been put in place to protect residents. These regulations cover a wide range of topics, from food safety to care practices. When a nursing home fails to meet a regulation, the inspection team issues a deficiency citation. There are a number of corrective measures that CMS can enforce when a nursing home is noncompliant. These measures include fining the nursing home, denying payment from Medicare or Medicaid, and assigning a representative to ensure that the nursing home takes corrective action. If the nursing home does not take corrective action, CMS may terminate its agreement, which would revoke the facility's Medicare and/or Medicaid certification. In that case, any residents who are beneficiaries of either program would be transferred to another nursing home.

According to several long-term care ombudsmen we spoke to, industry talk about nursing home inspections is common among area nursing homes. So while inspectors may show up unannounced, a nursing home may be prepared for the visit if the administrator is aware that other nursing homes in the area have recently been inspected. This makes your in-person visit that much more important. Your personal impression is a critical part of the process of choosing a nursing home. You don't need to be a professional inspector to learn a lot about a nursing home by visiting it.

One important note about deficiencies: they are not all equal. Deficiencies are essentially problems that, if they remain unresolved, have the potential to negatively impact residents' health and safety. In terms of their scope and severity, CMS distinguishes between deficiencies that have the potential for causing harm, those that actually cause harm, and those that place residents in immediate jeopardy. So when you review deficiencies, keep this in mind.

CMS' nursing home inspection results also detail how many residents were affected by the deficiency, reported as "few," "many," or "some," and what the level of harm is on a scale of one to four. Both of these components are useful measures for gauging deficiencies and understanding the results of a nursing home inspection.

According to the latest data available from Medicare, nine is the average number of nursing home deficiencies. With so many regulations, it's relatively common for facilities to have some deficiencies; you just want to be sure that the facility you choose is proactive about correcting mistakes and that none of the infractions are serious.

The top three categories of nursing home deficiencies in 2007 were accident environment, food sanitation, and quality of care, according to the Henry J. Kaiser Family Foundation on its www. statehealthfacts.org website.

Five Star Quality Rating System

In late 2008, Medicare instituted its "Five Star Quality Rating System" on Nursing Home Compare to help make the results of nursing home inspections easier for consumers to understand. The goal of the system was to provide an at-a-glance rating for each nursing home that summarized the inspection data.

Critics of the new rating system say that implementing an overall rating can be misleading because it oversimplifies nuanced information. Not only that, but the overall ratings can also be inaccurate, providing only a "snapshot" of how the facility performs during a particular period; for example, the quality measures, which are self-reported by the facility, can reflect residents' health for the week prior to the assessment, which may not be representative of their overall clinical measures.

Now that you understand how nursing homes are regulated and inspected, you know how important it is to understand the nature of specific deficiencies. So a word to the wise: don't rely on the five star quality rating system. Take your time to review all of the results for each nursing home on your list. That way, if you have any questions about whether certain issues have been resolved, you can write them down and take them with you when you visit the facility, and get the answers you need for your own peace of mind.

The Physical Visit

Even if the nursing homes on your list have positive inspection results, be sure to visit them in person. The quality of a nursing home can change very rapidly due to things like a change in ownership, management, or financial status. That's where the third and final step of choosing a nursing home comes in: visiting the facilities on your shortlist.

As with every senior housing option outlined in this book, we recommend visiting more than once. Make an appointment the first time so that staff is prepared to spend time with you, giving you a tour and answering your questions. For a follow-up visit, take a cue from the health inspectors and try dropping in without an appointment. This will give you an opportunity to see a more realistic side of life at the facility without the marketing spin. Try to visit once during mealtime and once during an activity, and if possible, sample the food and stay to observe (or participate in) the activity.

> Tour as many nursing homes as you can. It will help you get a feel for what to expect—and help you figure out what you do and don't like. On your visits, talk to residents, their family members, and staff. Ask questions that will help you gauge how happy they are at the facility.

On your first visit, check out the nursing home's activity calendar. Many facilities employ an activity director. Ask whether there are any activities that are not on the calendar. If you have timed a subsequent visit to coincide with a scheduled activity, verify that it takes place, and observe how the participants interact with each other. Do they look like they're enjoying themselves?

In addition to those who are participating in the activity, it's a good idea to pay attention to the rest of the residents you encounter on your visit. What's the ratio of short-term to long-term residents? This will inform the dynamic of the community, perhaps to a great extent. For example, are there many residents who come for rehab, stay a short time, and then return home? You may like the constant influx of new faces, or perhaps you will find it depressing. Either way, this is why it's important to find out what the resident population looks like before you move in. If, for example, you see a lot of younger, more active residents, this could change by the time you move in if they are actually there for a short-term stay.

Use commonsense to spot red flags. Do you see any residents who seem "out of it," who are obviously being ignored, or who are parked in a wheelchair simply staring off into space? If so, ask a staff member about it. Perhaps those residents are low-functioning and there is a good reason for what you think you are observing, but it never hurts to ask. And low-functioning residents can still benefit greatly from staying as engaged as possible. Remember: it could be you some day, so ask, ask, ask.

Checklist for Touring Nursing Homes

These recommendations are not inclusive, so use the checklists below to help guide you, and add your own questions as they arise.

Location

- ☐ Is the location of the facility convenient to your doctor, family, restaurants, shopping areas, and/or house of worship?
- ☐ Is parking available for your guests?
- ☐ How close is the facility to emergency (hospital) care?

Safety

- ☐ Is the facility locked at night? Are you comfortable with the level of security in the facility?
- ☐ If there is a separate dementia unit, is it locked? Are there door alarms? Does the facility use wandering precautions such as WanderGuard? (WanderGuard encompasses a host of technologies, from alarm systems to door monitors and wearable monitoring devices, which help prevent or curb dangerous wandering behaviors.)
- ☐ Is the facility prepared for natural disasters? Ask about smoke alarms, fire drills, and evacuation plans.
- ☐ Are there grab bars, handrails, and elevators in communal areas?
- ☐ Is the lighting adequate?

Rooms

- ☐ Are rooms private or shared?
- ☐ How are rooms assigned, or can you choose your own?
- ☐ Does the size of the room meet your needs?

☐ Can you bring personal furniture with you when you move in?

☐ Is there sufficient storage space for your personal belongings?

☐ Are all rooms or apartments equipped with smoke alarms, sprinklers, and a call system?

☐ Are there grab bars by the bed and in the bathroom?

☐ How clean are the bathrooms (if you would be sharing with another resident)?

☐ Can the bathrooms accommodate wheelchairs or walkers?

☐ Is there an unpleasant odor in rooms?

☐ Are personal belongings protected?

Staff and Management

☐ Do the staff seem friendly and helpful when they interact with residents?

☐ Do they introduce you to residents and encourage visiting with them?

☐ Do staff members appear to interact positively with each other?

☐ Are there staff members you can communicate with if you prefer speaking a language other than English?

☐ How many hours does the medical director spend at the facility per month? Is there another doctor on staff, and if so, how often is that person present?

☐ How do residents set up an appointment with the medical director or staff doctor?

☐ Will you have the same caregivers on most days? If not, how often will they change?

Residents

☐ Is the age, ethnicity, or faith of your neighbors important to you? That is, do you prefer interacting with people similar to you? If so, take note of the residents you encounter to determine compatibility.

☐ Do the residents you encounter seem well cared for?

☐ Do residents seem about as active as you?

☐ Do residents interact positively with one another?

☐ Do the residents seem happy?

Care

☐ Is the nursing home Medicare or Medicaid certified?

☐ What is the plan in the event of a medical emergency or hospitalization?

☐ Is there an on-site pharmacy, or will the facility arrange delivery service for prescriptions and necessary supplies (e.g., incontinence supplies)?

☐ How often are residents reassessed?

☐ What types of rehabilitative therapies are available?

☐ What are your options if you develop dementia after becoming a resident?

☐ Under what circumstances would the facility no longer be able to house and care for a resident? How is this determined?

☐ Does the facility have a hospice care contract?

Meals

☐ Are special dietary needs accommodated? Is there a dietitian or nutritionist on staff?

☐ Are snacks available in between mealtimes?

☐ Is there a communal dining room or restaurant(s)?

☐ Can you have meals delivered to your room, and if so, is there a fee?

☐ If you are able to sample a meal on your visit, is the food fresh and tasty?

☐ Will the facility store food that your family brings to you from home?

Activities

☐ Are you interested in the scheduled activities?

☐ Can residents suggest activities?

☐ Is daily exercise offered?

☐ Are worship services available?

☐ Is transportation provided for appointments, shopping, activities, and emergencies?

Facility Features and Aesthetics

☐ Is the indoor temperature comfortable? What about the noise level?

☐ Are there any unappealing odors?

☐ What amenities are available on site? (Examples include a beauty shop, activities room, fitness equipment, computer access, and outdoor gardens or patio.)

☐ Is there adequate access to common areas such as activity rooms and dining areas?

☐ Are the rooms and common areas appealing?

☐ Do the hallways and common areas accommodate wheelchairs and walkers? What about the residences?

Policies

☐ Is there a waiting list? How long is it?

☐ Is there a resident or family council or other organization through which residents can voice their views on the management of the community?

☐ Are pets allowed? What is the policy?

☐ What happens if you decide to move out, or if your health needs dictate that you must move?

☐ Can the facility terminate your housing agreement, and if so, under what conditions?

- ☐ What is the refund policy?
- ☐ What is the move-out policy?
- ☐ Is there a trial period for new residents? What is the policy?
- ☐ If you must leave the facility for a short time due to medical reasons (e.g., a hospital stay), will the nursing home hold your room for you? Is a reduced rate available during your absence?

Costs

- ☐ What are the upfront costs, including deposits and any other fees? Which of these are refundable and under what conditions?
- ☐ How often are fees increased? What are the criteria for increasing fees?
- ☐ How much do you get back if you move out?
- ☐ Which services are included in the basic costs? Get a copy of the fee schedule.

Notes

_____

_____

_____

_____

_____

_____

_____

_____

_____

_____

_____

_____

Before You Sign the Contract

Congratulations! You're nearly done. Now that you've completed the three basic steps to choosing a nursing home, there are just a few more things you need to do before making a final decision:

- Obtain a copy of the contract and review it with an attorney and/or financial advisor who is familiar with this type of contract and who can explain the terms to you. You can find an elder law attorney who specializes in this area through the National Academy of Elder Law Attorneys at www.naela.org.

- Ensure that all promises made verbally are stated explicitly in the contract.

- Read the facility's most recent state inspection report and review the deficiencies and citations. If you find complaints, follow up with facility management to ask how they have been resolved. You can also talk to your long-term care ombudsman, who will be able to tell you what kinds of complaints have been filed against the nursing home and whether they have been resolved.

- Get a copy of the fee schedule, a document that will tell you which services are included in the monthly rate and which services cost extra and how much. Use this document to help you compare costs at the facilities you're considering.

- Get the name and phone number or e-mail address of a person with whom you can follow up if you think of more questions later.

- Consider attending a resident council meeting (get permission first). Not only will this give you a good idea of what kinds of issues the residents have, but also how they are resolved. It's also a great opportunity to meet residents and ask for their opinions about the nursing home.

- Ask for a written description of the procedures for filing a complaint or grievance.

- Find out what the facility's policy is on preventative care. The older we get, the harder it is for our bodies to recover from illness. That is precisely why preventative care is so important in nursing homes.

- Get a list of resident or visiting physicians.

Chapter 8

Continuing Care Retirement Communities (CCRCs)

Originating nearly a century ago as a means of providing lifetime care to seniors who would assign their assets over in exchange, continuing care retirement communities (CCRCs) were initially church-sponsored organizations. Today, a number of CCRCs still have religious ties but many do not.

From urban high-rises to wide open suburban campuses that resemble upscale universities, the look of CCRCs is as varied as can be. In fact, people who begin to search for CCRCs are often pleasantly surprised to discover that what they always thought was a swanky apartment complex is actually a CCRC. Not to be outdone, the amenities at CCRCs are usually reflective of their upscale surroundings. Rather than the shared dining rooms found in independent or assisted living, for example, CCRCs are more likely to offer multiple restaurant-style dining areas with a variety of casual and formal dining options. Other amenities may include libraries, swimming pools, fitness facilities, walking paths, driving ranges, golf courses, and more.

The CCRC industry is in the midst of a large growth spurt. According to a joint report on senior housing construction trends issued by The American Seniors Housing Association (ASHA) and the National Investment Center (NIC) for the Seniors Housing and Care Industry, of the total CCRC construction projects in 2008, 63 percent were new properties, while 37 percent were expansion projects occurring on existing CCRC campuses. This surge in construction coincides with the graying of America's baby boomers, the oldest of whom will turn 64 in 2010. As the industry prepares for this influx of new residents and their lifestyle preferences, some new trends are emerging. These trends address boomers' views and preferences on life, work, health, travel, entertainment, technology, finances, and more. Studies show that boomers are working longer; traveling more; and demanding products, services, and technology that facilitate their active lifestyles. In recent years, many CCRCs have begun to focus on supporting residents' personal growth, such as pursuing new or lifelong hobbies, learning and giving back through civic engagement, volunteerism, and philanthropy. Boomers want to "have it all," and that's the golden promise that CCRCs extend.

What Is a CCRC?

CCRCs are a unique senior housing option that is based on a continuum of care. With convenient access to comprehensive services and different levels of supportive housing all in a single location, CCRCs enable residents to age in place, in familiar surroundings, as their needs change. Most CCRC residents enter the community at the independent living level and progress to higher levels of care as their needs change. Of course, this works both ways; for example, if a resident in independent living requires short-term skilled nursing, he or she may return "home" after making a recovery. While they provide support to healthy, independent seniors who want to maintain their current lifestyles, CCRCs also help residents prepare for the possibility of increased health care needs in the future.

The housing components of a CCRC may include all or some combination of the following:

- **Independent living** apartments (studios, one-, two-, or three-bedrooms)/condos, cottages, townhouses, duplexes, or single-family homes.

- **Assisted living** apartments may be separate or joined with independent living, in which case residents would have access to custodial care while residing in independent living apartments. Usually studios or one-bedrooms.

- **Dementia unit** freestanding or attached, locked dementia wing with specialized care.

- **Nursing home** shared or private accommodations. Usually a shared, furnished room.

Although CCRCs offer multiple levels of care and flexible housing arrangements, these communities are not designed for short-term residency. In fact, CCRC contracts usually specify that applicants are entering into a lifelong agreement with the community (although some contracts require a minimum of only a year). Most residents join at the independent or assisted living levels, while they are still healthy and active, and remain at the community for life, simply moving to higher levels of care as they are required. However, some CCRCs only accept applicants at the independent living level.

In addition, various communities may offer rental or purchase options. Purchase options involve the sale of real estate interest, meaning that you buy your accommodations. Like any other type of real estate, you would be able to will the property to an heir.

Finally, CCRCs may require residents to hold Medicare Part A and Part B coverage. Almost all require residents to have Medigap coverage, and some require long-term care insurance. Some long-term care insurance policies include coverage for some services provided at a CCRC. The type and amount of coverage will vary, so check your policy for details, and also check with the CCRC to verify whether it accepts long-term care insurance as a form of payment. CCRCs may also require residents to have certain up-to-date legal documents, which may include wills, living wills, and durable powers of attorney. You will find more information on these types of coverage in Chapter 10. Read more on legal documents in Chapter 14.

Many CCRCs are affiliated with religious groups, nonprofits, or other types of organizations. These affiliations may influence or even dictate the kinds of residents that the communities accept. For example, CCRCs with religious ties may accept only members of that religious group, or they may grant preference to those applicants while still maintaining an "open door" policy. Lifestyle can also play a part, with communities that focus on interests ranging from lifelong learning to culinary experiences, and others catering to specific groups such as the lesbian, gay, bisexual, and transgendered (LGBT) community.

Regulation and Accreditation of CCRCs

In some states, CCRCs are highly regulated. However, the absence of federal regulation means that CCRC services and offerings will vary from state to state.

The Commission on Accreditation of Rehabilitation Facilities and Continuing Care Accreditation Commission (CARF-CACC) is the only organization in the United States that accredits CCRCs. CCRCs are not required by law to be accredited, and the process of becoming accredited is very expensive; therefore, some communities elect to forego it. However, despite the lack of federal regulation and the fact that being accredited is not required by law, earning accreditation is significant because it means the CCRC has met strict standards for operation, financial performance, and resident care.

Regardless of accreditation status, there are some general requirements for CCRCs. At a minimum, for example, they must undergo annual financial audits and submit the results to their state's governing agency (usually the department of social services). The states set continuing care contracts statutes that help ensure that CCRCs have the financial resources to meet their contractual obligations to residents. These statutes are designed to protect residents from financial problems that the CCRC may experience. If the audit reveals that the CCRC is experiencing financial difficulties, the governing agency will require that the community take corrective measures.

Assisted living facilities and nursing homes that are part of a CCRC are subject to the same regulations as they would be otherwise. See Chapters 4 and 6 for more information on assisted living facilities and nursing homes, respectively.

Intake Meeting and Assessment

Every community will have different measures for determining your level of care, but in general, expect to move as your care needs increase. If you reside in independent living but require an increasing amount of help with the activities of daily living, for example, you may be transferred to assisted living. The same goes for a transfer from assisted living to skilled nursing.

Like assisted living facilities and nursing homes, CCRCs require applicants to undergo a comprehensive health assessment before moving to the community. The purpose is to determine the applicant's level of health and set expectations on both sides. The assessment may include a physical administered by a doctor of the community's choosing. Senior applicants who are independent but are physically frail, in declining health, or very elderly may be declined. There may also be limitations on coverage that exclude care for individuals with preexisting health conditions.

Levels of Care

All CCRCs offer a continuum of care, which typically includes independent living, assisted living, skilled nursing, and sometimes dementia and hospice care. Usually all of these are offered on the same campus, but that is not always the case. Some communities contract with outside care providers for the higher levels of care, such as skilled nursing, memory, and hospice care. It's possible that these services will be offered off campus, which would require you to move if you require access to these services. There is also the possibility that there will be no vacancy at the level of supportive housing you require when you are ready to transfer. CCRCs take measures to prevent this from occurring, but it would be impossible to predict each resident's progression of health care needs. Therefore, you must find out what kind of contingency plan the CCRC has in the event that this occurs.

Activities and Services

From convenience to activities, the kinds of services you'll find at CCRCs outrival those offered at any other singular senior housing option. Remember, with CCRCs it's not all about health care—it's about that promise of being able to enjoy your golden years with as little stress as possible. Certainly access to quality medical care is a primary factor, but so, too, is access to appetizing meals, appealing wellness programs, and enjoyable activities.

Some examples of activities that may be offered at CCRCs include lectures, movie screenings, art exhibitions, happy hours, field trips, and more. Classes are popular as well, with diverse topics ranging from computers to fitness to cooking. Residents often form groups to socialize with like-minded friends; book clubs and travel groups are common.

Every community will have different offerings, but you can expect the following basic services at most CCRCs:

- Access to an on-site doctor

- House calls during an illness

- Meal delivery during an illness

- Scheduled transportation

- Three daily meals in a choice of settings

- Housekeeping, linen, and laundry service

- A variety of social, recreational, and educational activities

- Community events

- Chapel services

Some of these services may be included in your contract, while others may incur additional fees.

Three Contract Types

There are three types of contracts used by CCRCs. They are known simply as Type A, Type B, and Type C. Each contract type is associated with a different level of risk to the resident and to the community. Residents assume the lowest level of risk with a Type A contract, and the highest level of risk with a Type C contract. For CCRCs, the opposite is true, where Type A represents the highest risk and Type C the lowest. The fee structures associated with each contract type correspond directly to the level of risk that each party assumes, but each type usually requires a one-time entrance fee as well as ongoing monthly fees.

CCRCs are not required to offer all three contracts. In fact, many communities offer just one or two. According to a 2008 study conducted by the American Seniors Housing Association (ASHA), an estimated 77.6 percent of CCRC residents use a Type A contract. This probably explains why many people use "continuing care" and "life care" interchangeably, although there is a distinction (see Type A and Type B contracts).

To make it even more confusing, these three distinct contract types may go by different names in different states. Not all states have each contract type, either. Regardless of which contract type you choose, however, one thing is the same: all three require long-term commitments, in some cases for life, so seek legal and financial counsel before committing to anything. If you sign a contract and break it later, you may be penalized and also may be forced to forfeit your entrance fee.

Type A: Extended Contract

Type A, or extended contracts, are also known as life care contracts. Perhaps you have heard the term "life care community." Life care communities are actually a subset of CCRCs that offer only Type A contracts. Originally, this was the only contract offered by CCRCs. Over the past two and a half decades, types B and C were developed to suit a range of needs and preferences.

Type A contracts require a significant upfront investment, but provide unlimited skilled nursing and health care services for life, with little to no cost increase. This contract is low risk for residents not only because it guarantees access to high-quality care, but it also helps residents budget for future health care costs. Increases may include the cost of additional meals and specialty medical supplies that become necessary. In general, life care contracts do not involve the purchase of real estate.

Earlier we mentioned that many CCRCs are affiliated with nonprofit organizations. In fact, an overwhelming majority—an estimated 97 percent—of CCRCs are run by nonprofits. Here is why that is important if you choose a Type A contract. While the rigorous financial screening process applicants must go through usually ensures that they will be able to meet their cost obligations to the community, occasionally residents run out of financial resources. When this occurs, many nonprofit communities will subsidize residents who become unable to pay for their housing or care.

Generally, nonprofit communities are in a better position than for-profit communities to provide continuous care to residents who outlive their financial resources and become unable to pay. This is because the funds may come from a number of sources, such as the sponsoring organization, charitable donations, and/or an endowment fund that has been set up for this particular purpose. By the same token, for-profit CCRCs are less likely to have similar resources and hence are less likely be able to afford these expenses.

Type A contracts require a higher entrance fee than Type B or C contracts because it covers the cost of care that the resident may require down the road. Making this initial investment can translate to significant savings over time, particularly when you consider that Medicare does not cover custodial care in a nursing home and provides very limited coverage of skilled care. Type A contracts are a great choice if you anticipate needing higher levels of care later on.

Type B: Modified Contract

A Type B contract is known as a modified or continuing-care contract. Like the Type A contract, the modified contract provides specified housing, services, and amenities with limited cost increases. However, Type B contracts limit access to long-term health care and nursing services. It works like this: the contract specifies a number of days (e.g., 30, 60, or 90) that the resident may access these services; residents who use those days and require additional care must then pay for the additional costs that are incurred. Some communities will discount the rates for residents with a Type B contract who have used care or services beyond the specified number of days, but others require the full cost. Type B contracts are a good choice if you do not expect your health care needs to increase significantly over time, and if you can afford to pay for health care that is not included in your contract.

Type C: Fee-for-Service Contract

The third type of contract is known as Type C, or a fee-for-service contract. It is designed for residents who want to pay only for care services they utilize. Like the other contract types, a Type C contract guarantees access to health care and residents receive housing, services, and amenities, which are specified in their contracts.

Some CCRCs waive the entrance fee for Type C contract users, instead charging only monthly fees. However, others opt to charge both an entrance fee and monthly fees. In some cases, the entrance fee may be held as a deposit from which the community withdraws funds to pay for the assisted living or skilled nursing care accessed by the resident, who would then be responsible for the full cost of any health care services used after the entrance fee fund had been depleted.

Type C contracts might be best described as the "you-get-what-you-pay-for contract." In the best sense, you literally only pay for the care services that you need, and only as you use them. Also fee-for-service agreements typically result in lower entrance fees (if applicable) as well as monthly fees. However, if your health needs change significantly and require long-term skilled care, you could be facing a considerable financial burden. Therefore, residents who opt for Type C contracts take the biggest risk, as they will be responsible for the full health care costs they incur.

Costs of CCRCs

Moving to a CCRC requires a serious financial commitment. With the exception of some Type C contracts, most CCRCs require a one-time entrance fee as well as ongoing monthly fees. Entrance fees may also be referred to as buy-in or purchase fees if they involve the purchase of real estate. Entrance fees may be fully, partially, or nonrefundable. This varies by community, so make sure you clearly understand the cost structure and rules regarding refunds. It is common for refunds to be returned on a pro rata basis to a resident's estate after he or she has passed, and this may be dependent on the re-occupancy of the resident's unit.

In general, buy-ins result in lower monthly fees as compared to rentals. Residents who move in at one level of care and move to an increased level of care, say from independent to assisted living, may have an increase of monthly fees, which will be specified in the contract.

There are several other factors that affect the fees that residents pay besides whether they own or rent their unit. These include the following:

- Contract type

- Size and location of the unit

- Services utilized each month

- Whether accommodations are shared or private

- Current health status (based on evaluation)

Monthly fees can start around $500 and may go up to $3,500 or more. Entrance fees start around $20,000 for a plan that does not involve the purchase of real estate, and can cost upward of $500,000 for plans where residents buy in. Obviously, these costs can vary greatly depending upon the variables. At one CCRC in the California Bay Area, the buy-in fee for a one-bedroom apartment costs between $329,000 and $495,000, with monthly costs of care ranging from $2,450 to $3,200 (add $1,500 for double occupancy). At the same facility, there is a one-time application fee of $250 per person, and as a resident, you can expect annual increases in monthly fees of between 3 and 5 percent.

You may be able to deduct a portion of your entrance fee and monthly fees as medical expenses. You will find more information on the tax benefits of CCRCs in Chapter 9.

Pros and Cons of CCRCs

CCRCs are a wonderful senior housing option in many ways. Not only do they offer you the opportunity to age in place in familiar surroundings, but in most circumstances you have guaranteed access to health care for life. Aging in place enables you to be part of a community that grows stronger over time, staying close to friends and loved ones who also live there. In this way, CCRCs are perhaps the best choice for spouses who are aging at different rates but want to remain close. In addition to all of these factors, it's the flexibility of housing arrangements, contract types, access to care, and superior amenities and services that make CCRCs a truly unique and adaptable housing option.

CCRCs are great, no question—if you can afford them. With Type B and C contracts, you run the risk of being faced with a significant financial burden if your health status changes unexpectedly and you are required to pay out of pocket for health care services. And no matter which contract you choose, you will most likely be required to make a lifetime commitment. It's also a very difficult and lengthy process—if it is even an option—to enter a CCRC at the assisted living level, as priority is usually given to current independent living residents. Indeed, many CCRCs only allow you to join the community at the independent living level.

Chapter 9

Choosing a CCRC

One might say that choosing a CCRC is a lot like getting married. Certainly there are parallels. For richer or for poorer, in sickness and in health—sound familiar? Like marriage, entering into a contract with a CCRC is a serious commitment: you want to choose the one that's right for you, one you can stick with for the rest of your life, one that's going to be there for you if you run out of money, and one that will bring balance to your life. In the case of CCRCs, that balance involves many factors: the location, services, and amenities; the quality of care; the cost; the culture of the community and its the operating philosophy; the living arrangements; and the community's financial status, just to name the basics.

Considering the Costs

First let's talk cost. Entrance fees are the most significant upfront cost when you move into a CCRC. You'll almost always be required to pay one, and they are usually refundable to some degree. Refunds may also be known as "rebates" in some states. There are three basic types of refunds:

- A **declining-scale refund** means that a resident's entrance fee is refundable on a declining scale over a period of time specified in the contract. 1 to 2 percent for each month of occupancy is typical. There may also be a processing fee with declining scale refunds.

- With a **partial refund,** the contract will indicate a certain percentage that is refundable upon specific terms, for example, if you leave the community or after your death.

- A **full refund** is usually the amount of the original entrance fee, less a fixed charge that is specified in the contract. Generally speaking, full refunds are associated with higher entrance fees than other refund types. The contract will also specify the conditions of a full refund.

The manner in which your entrance fee is refunded is important because it will help you answer the big question: can you afford it?

Getting a Feel for the Culture

You also need to determine whether the CCRC is a good fit for your lifestyle. If understanding the culture of another country is best understood by visiting that place and getting to know its citizens, then the culture of a CCRC is best gleaned from visiting in person and speaking with residents, their family members, and the staff who work at the community. While you can learn a lot from a CCRC's marketing materials, including what types of activities are offered and the amenities you'll be able to enjoy, nothing beats an in-person visit where you'll be able to put your five senses to work. Reviewing the marketing materials is exactly the same as reading a travel brochure—which, as you are probably well aware, can be a far cry from the real thing. So pack your bags and plan a trip!

The culture of a community and its operating philosophy go hand in hand. One of the ways in which this will affect you most is how the community shares information regarding its operations and finances with residents. In the CCRC industry, this is often referred to as "disclosure of information" or "information sharing." CCRCs may share information with residents through a resident council, formal reports, quarterly updates or meetings, or a combination of these methods. As an applicant, you have the right to review this information. You want to choose a community that is financially secure. And as a resident, you are entitled to this information on an ongoing basis so that you feel secure in the financial health of the CCRC—and your investment.

The purpose of exploring a CCRC's financial status is to understand whether it will be able to sustain itself over time and whether the community is stable enough to continue providing care to you for the duration of your contract. You may have already determined that you can afford a particular CCRC, but can it afford you?

Regulations vary by state, but typically CCRCs are required to disclose how they will be able to provide their contractual obligations to you. There are a number of financial performance indicators that can help you understand a CCRC's financial background and status, which may include a statement of financial position (also known as the "balance sheet"), a statement of operations, and audited financial statements. Request these documents and review them with your financial advisor.

The Physical Visit

You wouldn't rent a house without taking a tour of it first, would you? And most prudent buyers don't buy a home without a thorough home inspection. The same idea applies to CCRCs, whether you plan to buy or rent. Also it is imperative that you tour each of the levels of housing on your tour, not just independent living.

When you make an appointment to visit the CCRC, schedule a meeting with a staff member who is able to answer your questions about operations and finances. This will save you a lot of time.

Because CCRCs require such a long-term commitment, many communities allow potential applicants to try out the community during a short-term stay. This may range anywhere from a few days to a week or more. Ask whether this is an option. If it is, check it out. There is no better way to get a feel for daily life there. It will provide an opportunity for you to sample meals and activities, meet potential neighbors and ask their opinions about living there, and also begin to truly understand the culture of the community. Due to the significant cost associated with moving into a CCRC, most communities are happy to offer trial stays for potential residents and will usually pick up the tab, which includes accommodations and meals. The staff may arrange for you to have several meals with residents during your stay. Some CCRCs have a welcoming committee of residents who will greet you, introduce you around, and help you become acquainted with the community, while others will require that you attend a formal orientation meeting as well.

Are the CCRCs you are considering accredited by the Commission on Accreditation of Rehabilitation Facilities (CARF)? If they are not, you will need to conduct your own research into the facility's background, including operations and financial standing.

Checklist for Touring CCRCs

Use the following checklist to help you evaluate a CCRC on your visits and/or short-term stay.

Location

- ☐ Is the location of the community convenient to your doctor, family, restaurants, shopping areas, and/or house of worship?
- ☐ Is parking available for you and your guests?
- ☐ Is there access to public transportation?
- ☐ How close is the facility to emergency (hospital) care?

Safety

- ☐ Does the neighborhood appear safe? Do you like the neighborhood?
- ☐ Are you comfortable with the level of security in the facility? Is the front desk staffed 24 hours a day?
- ☐ If there is a separate dementia unit, is it locked? Are there door alarms? Does the facility use wandering precautions such as WanderGuard? (WanderGuard encompasses a host of technologies, from alarm systems to door monitors and wearable monitoring devices, which help prevent or curb dangerous wandering behaviors.)
- ☐ Is the facility prepared for natural disasters? Ask about smoke alarms, fire drills, and evacuation plans.
- ☐ Are there grab bars, handrails, and elevators in communal areas?
- ☐ Is the lighting adequate?

Residences

- ☐ How are apartments or rooms assigned once you require assisted living or nursing home care? Or can you choose your own?
- ☐ Does the size and location of the residence meet your needs?
- ☐ Will your furnishings fit, or are furnishings provided? Can you bring personal furniture with you if you have to move to higher levels of care (i.e., assisted living or skilled nursing)?

- [ ] Is there sufficient storage space? Can you reach the cupboards and top shelves?

- [ ] Is the kitchen equipped with a stove, sink, and refrigerator (i.e., can you cook and store food in your residence)?

- [ ] Are all rooms or apartments equipped with smoke alarms, sprinklers, and a call system?

- [ ] Are there grab bars by the bed and in the bathroom?

- [ ] Are housekeeping services available? How frequently?

- [ ] Are nursing home rooms private or shared?

- [ ] How clean are the bathrooms (if you would be sharing with another resident)?

- [ ] Can the bathrooms accommodate wheelchairs or walkers?

- [ ] Is there an unpleasant odor in nursing home rooms?

- [ ] Are personal belongings protected?

- [ ] Are residents allowed to smoke in their units? Are nonsmoking units available?

Staff and Management

- [ ] Do the staff seem friendly and helpful when they interact with residents?

- [ ] Do they introduce you to residents and encourage visiting with them?

- [ ] Do staff members appear to interact positively with each other?

- [ ] Are there staff members you can communicate with if you prefer speaking a language other than English?

- [ ] Is there a doctor or nurse on staff or on call in assisted living? What is the availability?

- [ ] Will you have the same caregivers on most days? If not, how often will they change?

Residents

- ☐ Is the age, ethnicity, or faith of your neighbors important to you? That is, do you prefer interacting with people similar to you? If so, take note of the residents you encounter to determine compatibility.

- ☐ Do residents seem about as active as you?

- ☐ Do residents interact positively with one another?

- ☐ Do the residents seem happy?

- ☐ Do the assisted living and nursing home residents you encounter seem well cared for?

Care

- ☐ What is the plan in the event of a medical emergency or hospitalization?

- ☐ Is there an on-site pharmacy, or will the facility arrange delivery service for prescriptions and necessary supplies (e.g., incontinence supplies)?

- ☐ How often are residents assessed?

- ☐ Is there a written service plan or care plan for each resident?

- ☐ What are your options if you develop dementia after becoming a resident?

- ☐ Under what circumstances would the facility no longer be able to house and care for a resident? How is this determined?

- ☐ What happens in the event that you develop a condition that the facility cannot provide adequate care for?

- ☐ Is the nursing home Medicare or Medicaid certified?

- ☐ What is the plan in the event of a medical emergency or hospitalization?

- ☐ What types of rehabilitative therapies are available?

- ☐ Does the facility have a hospice care contract?

Meals

☐ Are three daily meals included?

☐ Are special dietary needs accommodated? Is there a dietitian or nutritionist on staff?

☐ Are snacks available in between mealtimes?

☐ Is there a communal dining room or restaurant(s)?

☐ Can you have meals delivered to your apartment or room, and if so, is there a fee?

☐ If you are able to sample a meal on your visit, is the food fresh and tasty?

Activities

☐ Are you interested in the scheduled activities?

☐ Is daily exercise offered?

☐ Are worship services available?

☐ Is transportation provided for appointments, shopping, activities, and emergencies?

☐ Can residents suggest activities?

Community Features and Aesthetics

☐ Is the indoor temperature comfortable? What about the noise level?

☐ Are there any unappealing odors?

☐ What amenities are available on site? (Examples include a beauty shop, activities room, fitness equipment, computer access, and outdoor gardens or patio.)

☐ Is there adequate access to common areas such as activity rooms and dining areas?

☐ Do the hallways and common areas accommodate wheelchairs and walkers? What about the residences?

☐ Are the apartments or rooms and common areas appealing?

Policies

- ☐ Is there a waiting list? How long is it?

- ☐ If the facility is sponsored by a nonprofit organization (e.g., a church or university) and managed under contract to a commercial firm, what are the conditions of the contract?

- ☐ Is there a resident council or other organization through which residents can voice their views on the management of the community?

- ☐ What is the policy on overnight guests?

- ☐ Are pets allowed? What is the policy?

- ☐ What happens if you decide to move out, or if your health needs dictate that you must move?

- ☐ Can the CCRC terminate your housing agreement, and if so, under what conditions?

- ☐ What is the policy on medication administration?

- ☐ What is the refund policy?

- ☐ Is there a trial period for new residents? What is the policy?

- ☐ If you must leave the facility for a short time due to medical reasons (e.g., a hospital stay), will the nursing home hold your room for you? Is a reduced rate available during your absence?

- ☐ How is it determined that a resident must move from one part of the facility (as from independent to assisted living) to another?

- ☐ What is the contingency plan if there is no vacancy in the housing component you must move to? Does the community have a reciprocal agreement with another CCRC?

- ☐ If you run out of financial resources, will the community subsidize your costs?

- ☐ Does the CCRC offer any financial aid programs?

- ☐ Does the community disclose operational and financial performance with residents, and if so, what are the processes or methods for sharing information?

☐ Does the CCRC require applicants to obtain long-term care insurance prior to moving in, and if so, are applicants required to purchase a policy from a company recommended by the CCRC? If you are denied coverage, would the CCRC accept you if you met all other requirements?

☐ If the CCRC requires residents to purchase long-term care insurance through a recommended insurer, would your premiums be included in your monthly rate, or would you have to pay them separately?

Costs

☐ What are the upfront costs?

☐ How much is the entrance fee? Is it refundable?

☐ How are entrance fee refunds structured and what are the terms?

☐ What is included in the entrance fee?

☐ How much are monthly fees and how often are they increased? What are the criteria for increasing monthly fees?

☐ How are monthly fees affected when a resident must move to a higher level of care?

☐ If you move in with your spouse, what happens if your health care needs progress at different rates? If one of you must move to skilled nursing or passes away, how will the other spouse's rates be affected? Would that person be required to move to another unit?

☐ How much do you get back if you move out?

☐ Which services would be included in your monthly fees? Ask for a printed fee schedule.

☐ Are any of the costs that you would be responsible for covered by long-term care insurance?

☐ Are health, dental, and vision coverage included in the entrance fee and/or monthly fees? Ask for a detailed account of included coverage.

Notes

Before You Sign the Contract or Lease

You've visited the CCRC, perhaps even stayed there by now. You've taken the tour, spoken to the marketing people, talked with residents and maybe family members, and you've ticked off every checkbox on the touring checklist, so you're done, right? Not quite. You've still got just a few things left. Namely, getting answers to the following questions about how the community is run:

- Which contract types does the community offer? Are they lifelong contracts?

- Is the community for-profit or nonprofit?

- Are all housing and care components located on the same campus? If not, which components are located elsewhere?

- Is the CCRC affiliated with any type of organization? If so, what is the organization and nature of the affiliation?

- Does the community have a governing board? If so, how are board members selected?

- Does the CCRC have plans to build or acquire additional communities? Any development plans?

And the final two things that you must do:

- Ask for a copy of the community's most recent audited financial statements. Have a CPA review them to determine financial solvency.

- Have an attorney—preferably an elder law attorney who is familiar with CCRC contracts—review the terms, conditions, and requirements of the CCRC contract before you sign. You can locate an elder law attorney through the National Academy of Elder Law Attorneys at www.naela.org.

Chapter 10

Financial Planning

Much ado has been made about the wave—or should we say tsunami—of baby boomers flooding the senior housing market. Whether you agree that 60 is the new 50 or 80 is the new 60, one thing is certain: thanks to healthier lifestyles and advances in medical care, older adults are living longer than ever before. In many ways, longevity can be wonderful, particularly if you remain healthy and active, and can enjoy your golden years with family and friends, doing the things that you love.

But for many of us, advanced age is accompanied by health issues. Many people mistakenly believe that their private health insurance, Medicare, Medicaid, or some other "government program," will automatically cover the costs of their care if they become unable to pay. That is simply not accurate. In fact, many health insurance policies and Medicare usually don't pay for most (if any) long-term care expenses. And in order to qualify for Medicaid coverage, you must spend most of your savings and assets years in advance. With greater numbers of participants accessing Medicaid benefits and less funding from the federal government than ever before, Medicaid's five-year "look-back" period not only makes it more difficult for new applicants to qualify, but the process itself takes much longer, requiring more advance planning.

One of the most important factors in choosing the right senior housing option for your needs is the expense. The care and services associated with each option are also very important, but they won't matter if you cannot afford them.

The types of specialized senior housing discussed earlier in this book offer various types of support, health, and medical services. Because health care costs are so great, it typically follows that the more care you require, the higher the costs. Of course, there are exceptions. And there are also a number of ways to defray the costs.

It's never (ever!) too early to create a financial plan for paying for senior housing. In fact, the earlier you can do this, the better. We really cannot stress this enough: plan early and plan often. You'll be glad that you did.

Financial plans are as unique as the individuals for whom they are designed. Virtually all seniors use a combination of methods to pay for senior housing and care costs. Good financial plans are also dynamic and flexible. Your needs and expenses today will not be the same as they will be in 5, 10, or 20 years. The goal of creating a financial plan is to ensure that you have the funds to pay for your senior housing needs, whatever they may be, now and in the future. Ideally you will be able to protect and preserve your personal resources while taking advantage of programs designed to help share the cost burden.

This chapter will give you an overview of some of the most common methods of paying for senior housing costs, beginning with what to expect when applying to the various types senior housing.

Working With a Financial Pro

Unless you are a financial expert, we strongly recommend meeting with a financial planner—preferably one who specializes in working with seniors and who is familiar with senior housing and care costs—to draft your financial plan. Check out your advisor's credentials and ask for references. In addition to the person's credentials, keep in mind that there are many continuing-education programs to educate financial experts on the unique needs of seniors. Continuing-education credits show a commitment to staying "up" on changes in the industry. But beware of marketing hype. Aggressive marketing practices that target the elderly are extremely common.

There are many different types of financial professionals, and many will tell you that they specialize in one area or another. That isn't always the case, and if it is, they may have a conflict of interest. For example, insurance agents and stockbrokers can give you financial advice, and while it may be terrific advice, keep in mind that the nature of their jobs creates a potential conflict of interest, which may influence the advice you are given.

Make sure that the advisor you work with is a fiduciary. Fiduciary duty is a legal obligation for your advisor to only make recommendations that are in your best interests. Fiduciaries are held to a higher standard than other financial professionals. They are liable for the advice they give clients, which requires them to adhere to a high standard of conduct and trust, and be prudent in making recommendations. It is illegal for a fiduciary to misappropriate your money for his or her personal financial gain.

The Application Process

Long gone are the days where nursing homes were synonymous with retirement living. By now you know how great the differences are between the types of senior housing. So it should be no surprise that the application process for each type of senior housing arrangement is just as varied. All senior housing options require upfront screening to determine whether the applicants under consideration would make appropriate members of the community. This may include a health evaluation as well as a financial assessment and other considerations. This section will give you an overview of what to expect when applying to the different housing options.

Independent Living Communities

Because there are so many different types of independent living arrangements, there is no one-size-fits-all application.

The rental application process for seniors-only apartments is essentially the same as it is for any non-age-restricted apartment. Typically you will be required to pay a deposit (usually the equivalent of one or two months' rent), and show proof of income or otherwise demonstrate your ability to pay rent and utilities. For example, if you do not have sufficient income, you can qualify by showing financial statements or savings account statements from your bank. There may be associated costs for support services if available, as well as a fee if you break your lease.

If you are applying for subsidized housing, you will have to demonstrate financial need. The requirements and application process for each program varies. The high demand for housing assistance, coupled with rentals at below-market rates, and high occupancy rates with low turnover, all result in waiting lists that can run two years or longer.

Section 202 Supportive Housing for the Elderly is the preferred option (over Section 8 and public housing) because it is the only subsidized housing program specifically for low-income seniors. The application establishes that you meet age and income requirements. To further establish your eligibility, be prepared to submit the following documentation:

- Proof of income (e.g., tax returns)

- Medical and pharmacy bills (used to help calculate your rent)

- Contact information for your previous landlords for a tenant reference

- A statement from your doctor verifying that you are healthy enough to live on your own

Program eligibility for both the Section 8 Housing Choice Voucher Program and public housing is based on your age, gross annual income, family size (if family members will be living with you), and U.S. citizenship or eligible immigration status. You must also have proof of a positive tenant history or be able to provide personal references who can establish your suitability as a tenant. These two options do not grant priority to seniors based on age preference; financial need is the greater determining factor. Therefore, it is likely that you will face a long waiting list when you apply.

Because Section 8 is a tenant-based rental assistance program and you choose your own housing in the private market, the property owner must agree to rent the unit under Section 8, and the unit must meet minimum health and safety standards as determined by a HUD representative upon inspection.

The application process and eligibility requirements for planned independent living communities will vary by location. At a minimum, expect a process similar to the one described previously for senior apartments.

Assisted Living Facilities

Applying to an assisted living facility is fairly straightforward. At most places, the rental portion of the application is very similar to applying to a senior apartment. In addition to establishing your financial ability to pay, your overall suitability as a potential resident will be evaluated.

The application paperwork for assisted living is usually more extensive than it is for independent living. The following commonly appear on the application or supporting paperwork:

- Marital status

- Date and place of birth

- Primary doctor's name and contact information

- Any illness or condition (physical and emotional) that you have been diagnosed with or treated for in the last two years

- Previous senior housing residences, dates of residence, and reason(s) for leaving

- Durable power of attorney for health care

- Power of attorney

- Legal guardianship

- Medicare, long-term care insurance, and other health insurance coverage

- Life insurance, including the approximate and face values of the policy and beneficiary

- Sources and amounts of income

- Cash, real estate and investment assets, and amounts of each

- Liabilities

- Asset transfers that occurred within the last 36 months, including date(s) of transfer, amounts, and beneficiaries

The information that assisted living facilities are allowed to ask you during the application process varies by state.

Nursing Homes

Although the application process for nursing homes varies by state and facility, it is almost guaranteed that no matter where you apply, you will be asked the basic questions listed previously for assisted living facilities, in addition to more detailed questions about your health and finances. This information will help determine your eligibility for Medicaid.

First and foremost, to move into a nursing home, a doctor must certify that you require skilled nursing care. Most nursing home applications address the following points:

- Doctor's certification that you require nursing home care

- Documentation of payment plan

- Legal documentation of advance directives, living will, durable power of attorney for health care (and/or power of attorney)

- Any illness or condition (physical and emotional) that you have been diagnosed with or treated

- Name of prior nursing home(s), date(s) and length of stay(s), reason(s) for leaving

- Marital status

- Names of family members living with you

- Name and contact information for guardian/conservator

- Medicare, long-term care insurance, and other health insurance coverage

- Life insurance, including the approximate and face values of the policy and beneficiary

- Sources and amounts of income

- Cash, bank accounts, real estate and investment assets, and amounts of each

- Amounts and details of all other assets

- Liabilities

- Asset transfers that occurred within the last 36 months, including date(s) of transfer, amounts, and beneficiaries

- Detail of household expenses if you or your spouse owns your home

If you plan to use insurance to pay for your nursing home expenses, call your insurer to have your admission pre-authorized before you move in. The nursing home can assist you with obtaining a pre-authorization.

Nursing homes receive less money for residents whose care is covered by Medicare and Medicaid than they do for patients who pay privately, so for obvious reasons the latter is preferred. However, it is against the law for any nursing home representative to request that you pay privately rather than applying for Medicare or Medicaid coverage. If this occurs, report it your local ombudsman immediately.

At the time of admission, it is customary to receive the following:

- Information on how to apply to Medicaid and Medicare

- Residents' bill of rights

- Description of your legal rights as a resident

- Description of how to file a complaint

- Description of process for accepting or refusing medical treatment

- Instructions on how to contact your doctor at the nursing home (for family members)

- Fee schedule detailing services covered by the basic rate and services available for a fee

The contract or nursing home agreement will specify that the person who signs the document is responsible for all of the resident's expenses. The resident should always sign the agreement unless he or she has been legally been declared incompetent. Spouses typically have a legal responsibility for paying nursing home costs, but other relatives such as adult children do not—so avoid having them sign the agreement unless it is absolutely necessary.

CCRCs

People who choose a continuing care retirement community (CCRC) generally expect to live at the community for the rest of their life. So as you might expect, applying to a CCRC is a very involved process. And because many nonprofit CCRCs provide financial assistance to residents who run out of money, the application process is extremely thorough in order to minimize the facility's risk of taking on residents who are likely to outlive their resources. The process and requirements vary at each community, but basic requirements at most CCRCs include submitting proof of your financial ability to meet expected costs, meeting minimum insurance coverage requirements, and establishing proper legal documents.

CCRCs typically require detailed financial disclosure. You must prove that you are able to afford the entrance fee, monthly fees, and expenses at the level of housing you would enter into, as well as prove that you have sufficient funds for future fee increases or higher levels of care that may be required.

Many CCRCs require that residents have Medicare Part A and Part B coverage. Some communities may also require long-term care insurance and/or Medigap insurance, as well as a living will and durable power of attorney.

Protecting Your Assets

Senior housing can be incredibly expensive, particularly if you require long-term care. You've worked long and hard to earn the assets you own. If you don't take steps to protect them, you could face the scary prospect of using up your life savings to pay for housing and care expenses.

Fiduciary responsibility is not limited to financial professionals. Conservators, guardians, attorneys, and executors all have a fiduciary obligation to the person whom they represent. A fiduciary may be someone you hire for her expertise and knowledge on a particular subject, but it can also be a trusted relative or friend who you appoint to make important decisions on your behalf. An estate planner, tax expert, and trust lawyer are just some of the professionals with fiduciary responsibility who can help you as you draft your financial plan and determine your ability to pay for senior housing and care expenses. Part of their job is to give you advice how to handle your resources wisely; this includes helping you to preserve and protect your personal assets.

Identifying Your Personal Assets

Personal assets are essentially anything that you own, whether partially or outright, that has financial value. Here are some examples of common personal assets:

- Real estate
- Bank accounts/cash

- Pensions

- Annuity and investment income

- Vehicle(s)

- Insurance policies

- Shares/stock

- Businesses

- Jewelry and other valuables

Tax Considerations

There are a number of tax considerations that you should be aware of as you create your financial plan to pay for senior housing expenses. This book does not cover all of them in detail, but rather highlights some of the basic considerations, including property tax deferral and deferred-payment loans; tax credit for the elderly or the disabled; deductible medical expenses; tax credits for caregivers; and CCRC tax considerations.

A property tax deferral and deferred-payment loan are two methods of gaining access to funds using the equity in your home. A property tax deferral is a loan that you can use to help pay your taxes. The loan is based on your home equity and typically will not be due until you die or move out of your home. Contact your local property tax collector's office for more information and to see if you qualify.

Like a property tax deferral, a deferred-payment loan is based on your home equity and does not become due until you die or move out of your home. The funds from this loan are for making home repairs and improvements. Deferred-payment loans are usually available with no interest. For more information, contact your local area agency on aging.

You may have heard of the tax credit available to eligible seniors and disabled individuals, known as Credit for the Elderly or the Disabled. To qualify, you must be 65 or older, or if you are younger than 65, you must be retired on permanent and total disability. The credit is generally only available to U.S. citizens or residents who have an adjusted gross income, nontaxable Social Security, or other nontaxable pensions whose combined total is less than the amount specified for that tax year. For more information on current income limits and other eligibility requirements, download Publication 524, Credit for the Elderly or the Disabled, available at www.irs.gov. To determine the amount of the credit that you qualify for, you will need IRS Schedule R (Form 1040) or Schedule 3 (Form 1040A). Both forms are also available on the IRS website.

If you itemize your deductions when you file your income taxes, you may be able to deduct certain medical and dental expenses. If you are married and file jointly, you may deduct your spouse's expenses as well.

Allowable medical deductions apply to expenses paid for preventive care and treatment of both physical and mental conditions. Some examples of deductible medical expenses include the following:

- Fees paid to doctors, dentists, surgeons, and chiropractors

- Payments for hospital services, qualified long–term care services, nursing services, laboratory fees, and acupuncture treatment

- Cost of inpatient treatment at a center for alcohol or drug addiction

- Cost of prescription drugs (and also insulin)

- Cost of participating in a smoking-cessation program

- Cost of participating in a weight-loss program for a disease, including obesity, diagnosed by your doctor

- Cost of dentures, prescription eyeglasses or contact lenses, laser eye surgery, hearing aids, crutches, wheelchairs, and medically necessary guide dogs

- Transportation costs essential to your medical care, including fares for a taxi, bus, train, or ambulance; or, if you drive, either out-of-pocket expenses including gas and oil, or the standard mileage rate of 18 cents per mile (both methods allow tolls and parking fees to be deducted)

- Cost of meals and lodging at a hospital, nursing home, or other medical facility if your stay is for the purpose of receiving medical care

- Medical insurance and long-term care insurance premiums

You may only deduct medical expenses you paid during the tax year you are filing, regardless of the date of services. If you or your care provider receives reimbursement, you may only deduct the amount of the medical expense less the amount of reimbursement.

Your total medical expenses must exceed 7.5 percent of your adjusted gross income before you can make a deduction. Then you may only deduct the amount by which it exceeds that figure. For example, if your adjusted gross income is $100,000 and your total medical expenses equal $15,000, you may deduct up to $7,500. For more information and other restrictions, see IRS Publication 502, Medical and Dental Expenses. You can download this and other IRS publications for free at www.irs.gov, or call the IRS at 1-800-829-3676.

Many states provide a tax break for caregivers of the elderly. State tax credits, which are applied to your tax bill, range between $500 and $1,500. Tax deductions from the states may include approved caregiving-related expenses of up to $2,400. Tax breaks for caregivers are not currently available in all states. Check with your tax advisor for details.

If you are entering into a CCRC, you may be eligible for a significant tax break. The IRS allows CCRC residents to claim an itemized deduction of a portion of the one-time entrance fee (provided it is nonrefundable) and the ongoing monthly fees as prepaid medical expenses because they represent an investment toward future assisted living and nursing home care. Considering the expense of these fees at most CCRCs, they can easily add up to more than 7.5 percent of your adjusted gross income. The allowable percentage that you may deduct usually ranges between 25 and 30 percent, so this can result in significant savings. The allowable amount is computed on an annual basis by the facility; request this information. This itemized deduction is only available if you enter into a Type A (Extended) or B (Modified) contract, not a Type C (Fee-for-Service). (See Chapter 8 for an explanation of the different types of contracts.)

If you have the flexibility of choosing when you enter the CCRC and pay the entrance fee, you may be able to realize even greater savings. That is, the more monthly fees you are able to add to your deductible medical expenses for that year, the more you will save. Talk to your tax consultant to determine whether this is advisable.

If the entrance fee is wholly or partially refundable, in some instances that portion may be treated as a below-market interest-rate loan, and you may be required to pay imputed interest on it. There are certain exceptions to this: for loans of less than $163,000 (for 2006, the last year in which a figure was available) for loans that are refundable within a short period, typically six months. If the entrance fee is refundable, it does not qualify as a deductible medical expense.

In 2006, Congress made amendments to the tax code regarding imputed interest rules. These changes mean that most CCRCs that offer refundable entrance fees to residents are now considered exempt, and residents are not required to pay imputed interest. However, as of 2008, the IRS had not yet changed its regulations to reflect the amendments.

Tax laws are very complex, and are changing swiftly in the current economic climate. We strongly recommend meeting with a professional financial planner and a tax attorney who can help you plan your best course of action.

Spending Down

Spending down refers to the process of reducing your assets in order to qualify for Medicaid. Married couples are allowed various exemptions that are not available to single individuals.

Common methods of spending down to qualify for Medicaid include paying off debt, making home modifications, buying a car, and/or prepaying funeral expenses, all of which are allowed by Medicaid without penalty. Some methods of spending down, such as giving away assets, transferring property, and creating certain annuities, are allowed but may trigger a penalty.

Assets fall into one of three categories: exempt (assets that don't count), countable (assets that are subject to spend-down guidelines), and unavailable (assets that cannot be liquefied to pay for nursing home expenses).

Certain assets are exempt from spending down. For example, if you are single, your home is exempt if you intend to return to it. In some states, Medicaid assumes that you will not return home if you do not return within six months of being admitted to a nursing home, in which case your home would not be exempt. However, if you are married and either you or your spouse remains at home while the other is in a nursing home, then the home is exempt from spending down. The family car is also exempt if you are married and there is one at-home spouse (a.k.a. the "community spouse").

Community spouses qualify for a community spouse resource allowance, which means that they are allowed to keep 50 percent of the couple's assets, up to a predetermined maximum set by Medicaid. Those assets are exempt from spending down.

The amount of spending down that is required is based on your assets as a couple, as of the day that you or your spouse is admitted to a hospital, nursing home, or assisted living facility for an extended stay. This date is referred to as the "snapshot date." There is also a five-year look-back period, which means that Medicaid officials may review your financial transactions from the preceding five years to ensure that you meet Medicaid's eligibility requirements.

In order to qualify for Medicaid nursing home coverage, most states set the asset limit for single individuals at no more than about $2,000 in cash and other resources, excluding assets which are exempt. Applicants who have more than $500,000 in home equity may be declared ineligible for Medicaid.

As you can see, the process of spending down can be extremely complicated. Therefore, it is strongly recommended that you consult with professional Medicaid planner to design a Medicaid/Asset Protection Plan. This type of plan will help you "dispose" of assets in a manner designed to protect and preserve those assets for future expenses, such as funeral costs for yourself or your spouse. These funds can be converted to exempt status and protected from spending down.

Medicaid eligibility requirements are established by the states. Contact your state's department of health to learn the present asset limits where you live.

Converting Assets

One method of preserving and protecting your hard-earned assets is through a process that converts the assets from "available" to "unavailable."

Your home is a good example. Medicaid considers your home an exempt asset; in other words, it is unavailable. Many people who have cash but still owe money on their mortgage use the cash to reduce the amount they owe. This is one example of how to convert an asset—in this instance, the cash—from available to unavailable, by sinking it into an exempt asset like the family home.

Transferring Assets

Transferring assets refers to the process of giving away your assets. Medicaid planning routinely involves the transfer of funds to a trusted beneficiary. Once transferred, the funds belong to the recipient, who may hold or manage the funds to pay for health care costs not covered by Medicaid. There is obviously some risk inherent in the transfer of assets, so choose your beneficiaries wisely.

The transfer of assets is subject to a look-back period of 36 months of the snapshot date or the date that you applied for Medicaid, whichever is later. Certain transfers for trusts are subject to the standard five-year look-back period.

If the state finds that you have transferred assets for less than fair market value, you face certain penalties which include a $10,000 fine and up to a year in prison. In addition, the state is required to withhold payment for a certain amount of time known as the penalty period. The duration of the penalty period is variable. The formula divides the value of the transferred asset by the statewide average monthly private-pay rate for nursing home care. For example, let's say you transfer an asset worth $120,000 and the average monthly cost of nursing home care in your state is $3,000 for private-pay residents. That transfer could incur a penalty period of 40 months! There is no cap on the length of the penalty period, so you can see from this example how important it is to play by the rules.

Some transfers are exempt from penalty, including transfers:

- To your spouse
- To a third party for the sole benefit of your spouse
- To certain disabled individuals, including trusts established for those individuals
- For an approved purpose other than qualifying for Medicaid

Medicaid also reserves the right not to invoke a penalty period "where imposing a penalty would cause undue hardship."

Earning Income from Your Home

The number of senior homeowners in the United States has never been greater than now. And for many seniors, home equity is their most valuable asset. The greater the value of your home and the more equity you have built, the greater your options for earning income from your home. There are many different ways to earn income from your home. Some of the most common ways of doing this include selling your home, renting or sharing it, or taking out a reverse mortgage.

Selling Your Home

If you decide that selling your house is the best course of action, here is one thing to keep in mind. The Taxpayer Relief Act of 1997 entitles you to a capital gains exclusion. Single individuals may exclude up to $250,000 of the capital gains from the sale of a primary residence, and married couples may exclude up to $500,000. Those are the maximum amounts you are allowed to earn in profit from the sale of your home that are not subject to taxes. To qualify, you must have owned and used the home as your principal residence for at least two of the five years prior to the sale.

There are many things that you can do with the money you earn from the sale of your home. You can use it to finance a move closer to family or to a more agreeable climate, you can invest it so that you earn a continuous income and possibly build savings, and you can use it to pay for senior housing and care expenses. You may even decide to purchase a new, smaller home that is easier to maintain, perhaps in a senior community or CCRC.

Renting Your Home

If selling your home doesn't appeal to you, there are other alternatives. If you currently live there but are having trouble with keeping up with the maintenance, or if you don't live there but plan to return, or if you want to keep the home in the family or simply don't want to deal with the effort of putting it on the market—all of these are reasons you may want to consider renting your home.

There are many different scenarios for renting your home. For example, you can rent part of the house while you continue to live there, or you can rent it entirely if you reside elsewhere. If you don't want to deal with the responsibilities of being a landlord, you can hire an individual or a professional management company to do this for you. Either way, to protect yourself and to avoid misunderstandings between you and your tenant(s), it is advisable to use a lease that, at a minimum, states the basic terms of the rental. The income you earn from rent is taxable like any other income, but you may deduct a number of home-related expenses. Ask your tax adviser for details.

Sharing Your Home

Another alternative is sharing your home. Many seniors who find their home too big to live in alone or too troublesome to maintain on their own opt to share the space. If you are not comfortable renting a portion of your home to a stranger while you continue to reside there, perhaps you would be more comfortable sharing your home with family or a friend. It is your prerogative whether you choose to charge rent. If you decide not to, it is reasonable to ask whomever you choose to share your home with to help you contribute to the maintenance of your home and possibly share in household duties. Pooling your resources for groceries, utilities, and other shared household goods or services will help you both stretch your dollar.

Reverse Mortgages

You've probably heard of reverse mortgages. A reverse mortgage is a loan designed for senior homeowners that enables them to tap into their home's equity. The amount of the loan is based on the equity that you have established.

To qualify, you must be at least 62 and occupy your home as your primary residence. By law, before you apply for a reverse mortgage, you are required to undergo counseling by an independent third-party counselor approved by HUD. This is a consumer protection measure to ensure that you understand how reverse mortgages work and understand the financial implications and tax implications of entering into such an agreement. As part of the counseling process, you will also review alternatives to a reverse mortgage such as other home equity conversion options.

There are several ways to receive payments from a reverse mortgage. You can choose from a single lump sum of cash, regular monthly advances, or a line of credit. If you choose monthly payments, you have two options: tenure, which pays equal monthly payments as long you (or another borrower, such as your spouse) continues to occupy the home as a principal residence; and term, which pays equal monthly payments for a fixed number of months selected by the borrower. Many lenders allow borrowers to use a combination of payment types; for example, combining a line of credit with monthly payments. This is known as "modified tenure" or "modified term."

Obtaining a reverse mortgage will not affect your Social Security or Medicare benefits if you are receiving them. However, because Medicaid eligibility is based on income, if you are receiving benefits, the payments from a reverse mortgage could impact your Medicaid eligibility. See the Medicaid section later in this chapter for more information on eligibility requirements.

The benefits of a reverse mortgage are many:

- Tax-free payments as long as you live at home

- No payments due as long as you live in your home

- You retain the title and possession of your home

- Ability to choose a customized payment plan

- Flexibility to use money as you like, including paying off existing mortgage

- No prepayment penalty

- Amount owed cannot exceed the value of your home

Loan periods for reverse mortgages vary, but most guarantee lifetime tenancy, which means that you can remain in your home for life. The loan would become due when you (or your spouse, if you are married) die, sell your home, or move out permanently.

Reverse mortgages are not right for everyone. If you plan to leave your home within the next three years, you may wish to consider less expensive alternatives. You may be able to qualify for a home equity loan or no-interest loan, for example. A property tax deferral and deferred-payment loans are two other options to consider. Contact your local area agency on aging for more information on these programs and how you can qualify. You can locate your local area agency on aging by calling 202-872-0888 or visiting www.n4a.org for a direct link.

In addition, if you would like to leave your home to your heirs, a reverse mortgage may not be your best option, as it may need to be sold in order to pay off the reverse mortgage loan.

Government Assistance Programs

The federal and state governments have established several programs to help seniors pay for living expenses and health care after retirement. These include Social Security, Medicare, Medicaid, Veterans Benefits, Medigap, and PACE.

Social Security

Social Security provides supplemental income to retirees, disabled people, spouses and dependents of beneficiaries, and spouses and dependents of a deceased beneficiary. About 85 percent of each dollar you pay in Social Security tax goes into a trust fund that pays monthly to current retirees, their families, and to survivors of deceased workers. The other 15 percent is paid into a trust fund that pays benefits to disabled people and their families.

The future of Social Security is a hotly debated issue of late. The system has been under scrutiny for some time. Historically, Social Security has been a relatively simple system that required workers to pay taxes into the system, which used those funds to pay retirees. However, the biggest problem now faced by Social Security is that it is currently poised to begin paying out more benefits than it collects in taxes. If you are already retired, this will not affect your personal benefits.

When pressed for a ballpark figure, many financial advisors advise clients to plan for 70 to 80 percent of their work income for retirement. Social Security pays about 40 percent of an average wage earner's income in retirement, just to give you an idea of how it fits into the big picture. For most people, Social Security is just part of the picture. They also rely on a combination of pensions, savings, and investments to fund their living and health care costs.

During the years that you work, you earn "credits" that count toward your eligibility for Social Security. For 2009, you earn one credit for every $1,090 in earnings, with a maximum allowance of up to four credits per year. The amount of earnings equal to one credit goes up every year. Forty credits, which is equivalent to 10 years of work, is usually required in order to qualify for benefits. The minimum age for collecting benefits is usually 62. However, certain younger people may be eligible for disability benefits with fewer credits; the same is true for survivors of deceased workers.

Social Security benefits are not paid automatically. You have to apply for them. You also have the option of choosing when to begin receiving benefits. Social Security allows you to begin receiving benefits as early as age 62, but that is considered "early retirement" and if you choose this route, the amount of monthly benefit you receive will be reduced permanently. Your full retirement age depends on the year in which you were born. You can obtain this information by contacting the Social Security Administration. If you wait until your full retirement age to begin receiving benefits, you are eligible for 100 percent of your benefit. Different rules apply for primary beneficiaries and survivors or dependents.

If you receive Social Security benefits but have limited income and assets, you may qualify for assistance from Supplemental Security Income (SSI). SSI pays monthly benefits to qualified seniors 65 or older who are blind or disabled. Certain assets, such as the family home and car, are usually exempt and are not factored into the qualification process.

For more information, and to estimate the Social Security benefits you may be eligible for, visit the Social Security website at www.ssa.gov or call the toll-free information line at 1-800-772-1213.

Medicare

Administered and funded by the federal government, Medicare is a health insurance program for people 65 and older, certain disabled people younger than 65, and people of any age with end-stage renal disease. Medicare is divided into several subcategories known as Part A, Part B, Part C, and Part D.

The benefits associated with Part A are free and automatic once you turn 65. Part B is an add-on that requires a monthly premium. Enrollment in both plans is automatic if you file for Social Security benefits. If you do not receive Social Security, you may still enroll in Part A and Part B, but you may be required to pay premiums. You may opt out of Part B, but be aware that unless you are still working, there is a penalty for delayed enrollment; premiums are increased by 10 percent for each year that you are eligible but do not enroll.

Here are the benefits associated with each plan:

Part A: Hospital Insurance

- Inpatient hospital care (first 60 days minus first-day deductible; days 61–90 require daily co-payment of $267)

- Skilled nursing care (100 days, with certain restrictions)

- Hospice care

- Home health care (with certain restrictions)

If you are hospitalized, you must pay for the first day's costs. This is called the first-day deductible. Medicare offers 60 "lifetime reserve days," which enables you to extend a hospital stay past 60 days up to 120 days. Lifetime reserve days require a daily co-payment of $534 as of January 1, 2009.

Medicare's coverage for nursing home care is extremely limited. Medicare covers 100 days of nursing home care per illness, but you must meet a number of requirements before benefits will be paid. Coverage only begins after you have been hospitalized for at least three days, and only if you require skilled nursing care or physical, occupational, or speech therapy daily. In addition, only 20 days are fully covered; the remaining 80 days require a copayment of $133.50 per day (2009).

Medicare Part A covers home health care with some restrictions. Benefits do not begin unless you have been hospitalized for at least three days, and only if home health care is initiated within 14 days of your discharge from the hospital. Benefits are limited to 100 visits per illness.

Part B: Medical Insurance

- Doctors' services

- Physical, occupational, and speech therapies

- Pathology

- Clinical social worker services

- Clinical psychologist services

- Outpatient hospital care

- Rural health clinic services

- Outpatient rehabilitation facility services

- Ambulance services (limited)

- X-ray treatment

- Radiation treatment

- Home health care not covered by Part A

- Mammography screening (limited)

- Certain injectable drugs (limited)

- Durable medical equipment

There is an annual deductible of $135 for Medicare Part B. Medicare has fixed fees that are sometimes referred to as allowable or approved charges; these amounts are often substantially less than the actual charges. When there is a discrepancy, Medicare reimburses 80 percent of allowed charges; you are responsible for the balance.

As of January 1, 2009, the basic Part B premium is $96.40 per month. If you are single and your income exceeds $85,000 or if you are married and your combined income exceeds $170,000, your premium may be more. In addition, here are the copayment amounts for 2009:

- Inpatient hospital deductible: $1,068

- Inpatient hospital co-payment for days 61–90: $267 per day

- Hospital co-payment for days 91–150: $534 per day

- All costs for each day beyond 150 days

- Nursing home co-payment for days 21–100: $133.50 per day

Part C: Medicare Advantage

- Medical savings accounts

- Coordinated care plans—private health care plans provided by preferred HMOs, POSs, PPOs, and PSOs

Medicare Advantage was formerly known as "Medicare+Choice." If you are entitled to Medicare Part A and are enrolled in Part B, you are eligible to switch to a Medicare Advantage plan, but you must reside in the plan's service area.

Part D: Prescription Drug Coverage

• Individual plans are available through Medicare-contracted insurance companies

Medicare Part D is offered through insurance companies and other private companies that contract with Medicare. There are a number of plans available, and your costs will depend on the plan you choose.

You may have heard of something called the "donut hole," which is associated with Medicare Part D. This refers to a coverage gap for certain medications not covered by the plan. If you require medications that fall within the donut hole, you must pay 100 percent of the cost.

Beginning January 1, 2010, drug plan sponsors under Part D will be required to use the amount you pay to the pharmacy to determine cost-sharing amounts and for reporting the drug costs of plan to the Center for Medicare & Medicaid Services. Currently, drug plan sponsors are allowed to pass on administrative costs, which are reflected in the higher prices paid by beneficiaries.

Medicaid

Jointly funded by the state and federal governments, Medicaid is a health insurance program for low-income individuals and their families who are unable to meet health care expenses on their own. Medicaid is the largest source of funding for health and medical coverage for low-income people in the United States. It pays for about half of all nursing home costs in the United States.

Each state operates its own Medicaid program; program names and eligibility requirements and coverage vary by state. To be eligible, you must meet certain income and asset limitations. However, that alone will not qualify you. Other eligibility factors include whether you are elderly, disabled, blind, and whether you are a U.S. citizen or lawfully admitted immigrant.

If you receive Social Security benefits and you qualify for Medicaid, a portion of your Social Security funds will be allocated toward your medical expenses. Apart from this deduction, Medicaid covers most medical expenses.

Until recently, Medicaid used to pay 100 percent of medical expenses for beneficiaries, but on November 25, 2008, a new federal rule was passed that allows the states to charge higher premiums and co-payments to program participants. These fees are based on a sliding scale not to exceed 5 percent of the family's income. This new cost-sharing rule was enacted to help the federal and state governments save money through sharing the costs with program participants, who, in turn, were anticipated to reduce the services they accessed, using benefits for only medically necessary care.

Medicaid primarily pays for nursing home expenses, but some states offer waiver programs to help seniors who qualify pay for assisted living costs. This is referred to as the Medicaid Assisted Living Waiver. Coverage is variable depending upon your eligibility and availability of the program where you live. Contact your local area agency on aging for more information.

Veterans Benefits

The Department of Veterans Affairs (VA) administers a benefits package for veterans and eligible family members. Veterans benefits cover primary and preventative care, including hospital and outpatient medical care. There are eight priority groups, or levels of priority, to ensure that veterans with the greatest medical and financial need are prioritized. Veterans with a service-related disability and veterans who fall below the low-income threshold have top priority.

To be eligible for care, you must be enrolled in the VA health care system. Although no monthly premium is required for VA care, an annual financial assessment may be required to determine the priority group that you are eligible for and whether you qualify for free services. Veterans whose household income and net worth exceed the established threshold may be required to meet a deductible and agree to co-payments to become eligible for VA health care services.

The Uniform Benefits Package available to all enrolled veterans includes the following:

- Inpatient hospital care

- Ambulatory care

- Emergency care in a VA facility

- Home health care

- Prescription drugs and pharmaceuticals

- Durable medical equipment (e.g., wheelchairs and hospital beds)

- Adult day health care

- Diagnostic and treatment services

- Rehabilitation

- Mental health services

- Substance abuse treatment

- Prosthetic equipment

- Respite and hospice care

If you have health insurance or are eligible for other health care programs such as Medicare, Medicaid, or TRICARE, you may use those services in conjunction with your VA benefits. In fact, the VA recommends maintaining your current coverage so that you have as many options available to you as possible; the funds for VA benefits are limited and the number of enrollees is on the rise.

The VA has its own facilities for assisted living and skilled nursing care, although in some circumstances, eligible veterans may qualify to receive care in a non-VA facility.

The VA offers an Aid and Attendance Benefit to help pay home care, assisted living, and nursing home expenses for veterans and surviving spouses. To be eligible for the Aid and Attendance Benefit, you must be eligible to receive a pension, and require custodial care, be bedridden, be a patient in a nursing home, or be blind (or nearly blind). Single veterans are eligible for up to

$1,632 per month, surviving spouses are eligible for up to $1,055 per month, and couples are eligible for up to $1,949 per month as of 2009.

Medigap

Also known as Medicare Supplemental Insurance, Medigap is a type of health insurance policy that was created to address the coverage gaps in the original Medicare plan, such as coinsurance, deductibles, and co-payments required by Medicare. Medigap policies are sold by private insurance companies. There are 10 types of Medigap policies; most cover the co-payment for days 21–100 in a skilled nursing facility, but none pay for long-term care in a nursing home.

Although the federal and state governments regulate the coverage offered by all 10 Medigap policies, be aware that you may find policies that offer identical benefits at different rates. Not all companies offer all 10 policies, either. So shop around and compare policies before you buy.

In order to qualify, you must be a recipient of both Medicare Part A and Medicare Part B, and cannot be on Medicaid. Spouses must purchase separate policies.

For more information, to learn how Medigap policies work and how insurance companies set prices for Medigap policies, read Medicare's guide entitled "Choosing a Medigap Policy: A Guide to Health Insurance for People with Medicare," available for download at www.medicare.gov. Click on "Find a Medicare publication." The guide also details coverage for all 10 Medigap plans.

Programs of All-Inclusive Care for the Elderly (PACE)

PACE is a program run by Medicare. It provides continuous care and services for seniors and disabled people 55 or older who require skilled nursing care, with the goal of delaying nursing home placement and enabling program participants remain at home or continue living in the community for as long as possible. PACE is essentially considered an alternative to nursing homes, although the program will provide coverage for nursing home care when necessary. Care is coordinated and provided by an interdisciplinary team of professionals.

As a Medicare program, PACE provides the same coverage for care and services as do Medicare and Medicaid, in addition to medically necessary care and services (approved by the interdisciplinary team) not covered by Medicare and Medicaid. If you become unable to pay, you will still be able to receive benefits. You may opt out of PACE at any time.

Coverage includes the following:

- Primary care (including doctors' and nursing services)
- Adult day dare
- Home care
- Social services
- Laboratory and X-ray services
- Hospital care
- Medical specialty services
- Prescription drugs
- Nursing home care
- Emergency services
- Physical, occupational, and speech therapies
- Recreational therapy
- Meals
- Dentistry
- Nutritional counseling
- Social work counseling
- Transportation

To be eligible, you must meet the following requirements:

- Be at least 55 or older
- Live within the service area of a PACE program

- Have a certification from the state attesting to your need for skilled nursing care

- Be able to live safely at home, with assistance from PACE

Long-Term Care Insurance (LTCI)

Long-term care insurance is sold to individuals by private insurance companies. Some employers offer group long-term care insurance plans to employees. The benefits depend on the type of long-term care insurance policy that you purchase.

The following services may be covered, depending on your policy:

- Custodial care in your home

- Adult day care

- Adult day health care

- Care in an assisted living facility

- Care in a skilled nursing facility

Generally, the younger and healthier you are when you apply for a long-term care insurance policy, the lower your premiums will be. If you are in your 70s or older and you have health issues, you may be considered too high-risk for long-term care insurance and you may not be able to qualify for a policy. If you do qualify, the premiums can be extremely expensive. Some long-term care policies have restrictions on age and health status. Applying for long-term care insurance earlier, such as when you are in your 50s or 60s, you're more likely to be eligible for a policy based on your age and health status, assuming you have no serious health conditions. These factors may also qualify you for lower premiums.

Long-term care insurance certainly isn't the best choice for everyone. But if you can qualify for a policy and afford the premiums, it may be a great option to consider. Long-term care insurance can help you protect your assets and ensure that you will be able to pay for long-term care services without depleting your savings.

The biggest downside of long-term care insurance is undoubtedly the cost. It's expensive. A good rule of thumb: don't buy a policy if the cost of premiums will cause you to sacrifice things that are important to you now. If you do decide to purchase a policy, make sure you can comfortably afford the premiums, even if your income declines. If you don't pay your premiums when they are due, you run the risk of the insurer canceling your policy.

Long-term care insurance policies are very customizable. You build your own policy based on the following factors that are important to you.

Coverage

There are three basic types of long-term care policies to choose from: home care only, facility only, and comprehensive. Home-care-only policies pay for care at home and also cover adult day care and adult day care services provided. Facility-only policies pay for care in an assisted living facility and nursing home. Comprehensive policies pay benefits for all of these options.

Daily Benefit

This is the amount of money the insurer will pay out in benefits for each day you require long-term care services covered by your policy. Expenses that exceed the daily benefit must be paid out of pocket.

Benefit Period

This refers to the length of time your policy will pay benefits. Benefit periods offered by insurers may be anywhere from a specific length of time, such as three to five years, or you may choose a lifetime/unlimited benefit.

Elimination Period

This is a period in which all long-term care expenses must be paid out of pocket. The elimination period functions similarly to a deductible; rather than the policy dictating a dollar amount that you must spend before benefits will kick in, however, you specify a waiting period. Elimination periods of 30, 60, and 90 days are the most common, but a longer period could be set at up to 365 days. Like a deductible, the greater the elimination period, the lower your premiums.

Inflation Protection Benefit

This is one of most important features of a long-term care insurance policy, but also one of the most complicated. Inflation protection will help your coverage keep pace with rising health care costs. There are several options to choose from: no inflation protection, a future purchase option (you can add inflation protection later by paying higher premiums), or automatic inflation protection (your daily benefit increases annually without triggering premium increases).

Nonforfeiture Benefit

This means that your policy will continue to pay for your care even if you become unable to pay the premiums. You'll pay for it, though: the nonforfeiture benefit can add 10 percent to 100 percent to your premium.

Premium Payment Period

Most insurance carriers offer three choices of payment periods: lifetime, pay to a certain age, or pay for a certain timeframe. You may choose between several options for paying your policy premiums. The two basic methods are the continuous payment option and the limited payment option. The continuous payment option is the most common method that people choose. It requires payments of premiums at regular intervals, usually for your lifetime, or until you begin receiving benefits. If you stop receiving benefits, you would have to resume making premium payments. Your policy cannot be canceled unless you fail to pay your premiums on time. If you choose the continuous payment option, it usually results in lower premiums.

The limited payment option enables you to limit the period in which you pay premiums, either for a predetermined number of years or up to a certain age. A few commonly used methods of limited payment include single pay, which requires a single lump-sum payment; 10 or 20 pay, which covers a period of 10 or 20 years; and pay to 65, for which you must be younger than 65 to qualify. No matter which of these options you select, the limited payment option is usually more expensive. The benefit of selecting this option, because it allows flexibility of paying earlier, can be useful if you anticipate a drop in income after your premium payment period. It can also enable you to take advantage of certain tax deductions. Keep in mind that not all insurance carriers offer every payment option.

Financial Strength of the Insurer

Finally, in selecting a long-term care insurance company, one of the most important steps is to evaluate the company's financial strength. Two methods of doing this include investigating the company's reputation and checking its claims-paying history. You want to be sure that your benefits will be paid you if you must file a claim.

You can research the financial strength of long-term care insurance carriers through the five major rating services: A.M. Best, Duff & Phelps, Moody's, Standard & Poor's, and Weiss Ratings. See Appendix C for contact information for these services. Contact your state department of insurance for details on specific long-term care insurance carriers. You can find your state department of insurance by calling the National Association of Insurance Commissioners at 202-471-3990 or visiting www.naic.org for a direct link to your state.

Private Funds

You may have heard of the term "private pay" or "private payment." This simply means that you pay expenses out of pocket with your personal funds. The majority of newly admitted nursing home residents, for example, pay privately until they run out of resources and become eligible for Medicaid. Private payment may consist of a variety of income sources, including employment, pensions, Social Security, and investments.

Sometimes long-term care insurance is considered private pay because it is a nongovernmental source of payment that you acquire on your own. When insurance and other payment sources do not cover your full costs, you will most likely be responsible for paying the balance out of pocket. That is why it is so important to have a clear understanding of all costs and financial obligations from the beginning.

Not sure where to start? Even if you are financially savvy, this is a lot of information to take in. To gain a solid understanding of a complicated program like Medicaid requires a lot of research and, in the end, you may end up with more questions than you started out with. There are countless publications and websites explaining how these programs work, and that alone can be overwhelming.

BenefitsCheckup, a nonprofit website maintained by the National Council on Aging, is a great place to start. With information on more than 1,650 public and private benefits programs, you can find sources of financial assistance for lots of different things, from prescription medications to rent and utilities. Learn more at www.benefitscheckup.org.

Another great place to start is with your State Health Insurance Assistance Program (SHIP). Funded by the federal government, SHIPs have trained volunteer counselors who are well versed in common insurance issues and can help you resolve problems and answer questions about Medicare, Medicaid, Medigap, long-term care insurance, and other types of health insurance. While SHIP volunteers cannot recommend specific policies to you, they can help you determine whether you can streamline your existing policies (e.g., if you have separate policies with the same benefits). Counseling is free, and there are SHIPs in all 50 states. Call your local area agency on aging for the number where you live, or go to www.medicare.gov and search for "SHIP."

Chapter 11

Sorting Through Your Choices

Nearly everyone who has been through the process of finding and paying for some type of senior housing and services will be able to give you personal advice and opinions on how you can do it, too. And while they might have valuable advice, it's important to remember is that no two situations are the same. Your friends and neighbors are a great source for advice, but don't let them be your only source. You may qualify for benefits and programs that they don't, or which they don't know about. Also lots of important factors that will influence your decisions about senior housing change over time—tax laws, regulations, and facility owners, just to name a few.

Choosing a senior housing residence is much more involved, and more nuanced, than simply picking a name from a list because it's the cheapest, or closest, place on there. Doing so is simply playing roulette with your future. Being knowledgeable about your options and realistic about your situation is imperative in choosing the best senior housing option for your needs. Although in many situations, there is no one "right" choice, there is usually an option that will best fit your unique needs and preferences.

For example, you may be able to choose between receiving home health care in your home or moving into a nursing home. If you have a long-term care insurance policy that pays a home health benefit in your home, then it might make sense for you to stay there. But if you don't, and you qualify for Medicaid, then you might choose to move into a nursing home, especially if it means you will be closer to family and friends who can visit you regularly. If you choose the nursing home, you would have considerably less privacy than you would if you remained in your home and opted for home health services. You see where this is going, obviously.

Choosing senior housing that fits your needs and your lifestyle involves striking a balance between quality of care and quality of life, two extremely important considerations. Finding that balance is no easy task. But it is possible.

This may be one of the most important decisions you will ever make. It's so much more than a simple matter of where you live; it involves your health, your spiritual and social well-being, your finances, and, in many cases, your family. The best advice that we can give you is to plan early and, if you can, well in advance of the time when you need to move.

Evaluating Your Options

To find a senior housing residence that suits your needs, first you need to determine what those needs are. We strongly recommend getting an assessment. An assessment is sometimes called a needs assessment or geriatric assessment. It is a comprehensive status review of your physical and mental health, physical environment, and financial state. An assessment may also address psychosocial needs by determining your personal goals and values. Assessments can also identify potential risks and ways to avoid them. Using this information, you can create a list of senior housing options, determine what you can afford, and begin looking for facilities that might be a good match for your needs, preferences, and budget.

There are a number of ways you can go about getting an assessment. Geriatric care managers routinely perform assessments, and your doctor may be able to assist with some aspects. You may find a geriatric assessment center by calling your local hospitals. And you can always call your local Area Agency on Aging for a recommendation on where to go for an assessment.

No two people will have the same experience at a residence even when they have the same basic accommodations, opportunities, and services afforded them. While this is partly due to personal expectations, it is largely reliant on how engaged you are in making choices that involve you. This is why an assessment is so important. It will paint a clear and complete picture of the things that you need now, and it will prompt you to think realistically about the things you might need in the near future. You are an advocate for yourself and what you need. It's unrealistic for even the best senior residences to meet a new resident's every need, and meet high expectations, when the resident doesn't know her needs or isn't able to communicate them. You will have a significantly different—and much more positive—experience if you and your family are actively involved in your care from the beginning.

Reviewing the Basics

Once you have a list of senior housing options, start narrowing it down by comparing the basic considerations, including services, location, and costs. Then visit those places in person. Book an appointment with the administrator. Bring this book with you, and refer to the questions and the touring checklists found in previous chapters. Talk to residents. Go more than once and at different times of day. For example, you might plan to go during a scheduled activity and then have a subsequent visit coincide with a meal, preferably lunch or dinner. Is the dining room full, or are most people eating in their rooms? Make an appointment for the first visit and get the official tour. Then drop by for a second visit unannounced.

If you are visiting nursing homes, you might consider planning a morning visit. Drop by before 11:00 A.M. if you can. Are residents up and out of bed? If not, it might be an indicator that the facility is understaffed. (Keep in mind that residents have a choice of when to get up—but 11:00 is fairly late even by late-riser standards. This could indicate something else altogether, like depression.)

Is the residence senior-friendly? Even if you have no trouble getting around now, consider possible mobility limitations in the future and look at the furniture and facility layout with a critical eye. If it is a multi-level facility, is there an elevator? Are doorways wide enough to accommodate a wheelchair? Are there grab bars in the bathrooms near the shower and toilet?

Ask the administrator how long she has worked at the facility. What about the director of nursing and the medical director? A lengthy tenure is an excellent indicator of stability. All senior housing functions best when the facility is run well from the top down. Nurses, caregivers, and other staff feel the effects of a strong, stable management team just as strongly as they are bound to feel the effects of one that is variable or unpredictable.

If the administrator or other high level staff member is relatively new on the job, it's not necessarily a bad thing. In fact, sometimes bringing in new leadership is a very positive change. But be prepared for bumps; it takes a while for everyone to get used to new policies or a new management style.

Who is the owner? Is it an independent nonprofit facility or part of a corporate chain? Has the facility recently changed owners or is new ownership pending? These details can be significant if there have been complaints filed against the facility in the past; many past grievances are not as meaningful when a new owner has since taken (or is about to take) over.

Whatever type of senior housing arrangement you are considering, there will be at least one staff member whose job it is to follow up with you. It's good customer service to contact you to see if they can be of further assistance or answer any questions that you may have, but it should be done in a respectful manner, not a pushy one. People have their jobs to do, and sometimes part of the job in senior housing includes renting units and filling beds. This shouldn't affect your decision one way or the other. Recognize pushy tactics for what they are: pushy tactics. Don't let a marketing associate bully you into making a decision.

As you're considering different senior housing options, also consider ancillary services that could be utilized in order to make various housing options a better fit. These services could include home care, home health care, adult day care, adult day health care, senior centers, and more. Keep your mind open to blended solutions.

Comparing Choices

After you've visited the senior housing residences on your shortlist, it's time to compare these options to each other. Just as you did before, make the comparison easier by breaking each residence down into a series of simpler tasks: compare objective measures such as location, size, cost, type, and scope of services offered. Then repeat the process, but this time make notes on subjective lifestyle considerations, including offered activities, residents' level of activity/mobility, cultural, fitness, and social opportunities. This will make it easier to assess the big picture.

Also ask: what if your needs change? Can you bring in outside caregivers? What are the policies regarding private caregivers? What kind of special needs is the facility equipped to handle (e.g., chronic or terminal illness, or dementia)? If you develop special needs, would you be forced to move again?

Make note of any concerns you have about a particular facility. Discuss these concerns and any other remaining questions you have with your contact at the facility.

Where to Get Information, Support, and Advice

You should discuss each option with people you respect and whose opinion you trust. These advisors may include personal contacts such as family, friends, your doctor, your pastor or rabbi, and other people from your place of worship; they may also include professionals such as a geriatric care manager, social worker, hospital discharge planner, financial planner, or long-term care ombudsman. Ultimately, this is your decision. There are no rules on where to go for information, support, and advice on choosing senior housing. There is only one basic guideline: seek counsel from trusted sources.

It's not only the process of learning about, finding, and selecting the senior housing options that meet your needs that is a struggle; it's also dealing with the emotional outcomes of your decision. Frustration, guilt, anger, confusion, and uncertainty are all common for both new residents and their families. If you are leaving a spouse, it can be especially difficult.

After moving in to senior housing, feelings of insecurity and depression are common in new residents. Family members can help you through this struggle by reassuring you that they are still there to support you when you need them. Fellow residents and staff members are also quite experienced in the emotional implications following a move to senior housing. They can help, too, if you let them.

There are many experienced professionals in the senior housing, senior care, and aging services industries who are knowledgeable in these matters, and whom you can turn to for guidance in choosing a senior housing residence. Seek help when you are not sure what to do.

Hospital Staff

Hospitals employ staff members to work with patients who require care after they are discharged. These employees are usually called hospital discharge planners, but may also be known as discharge coordinators, medical social workers, or case managers. Discharge planners often have a background in medical social work. Their role is to help you transition from hospital to home or another setting as appropriate for your situation. These individuals work together with your doctor to assess your immediate needs and suggest facilities or services (such as home health care) as appropriate. They will give you specific recommendations on where to go, but we suggest doing your own research into the validity of these recommendations.

Hospital discharge planners are very knowledgeable about local senior housing options and community services, and are an excellent professional source to turn to for information and advice. They can answer questions you have about the care you are receiving in the hospital as well as what type of care you will need once you are discharged and where to go to get it.

If you believe that you are being prematurely discharged from the hospital, you have the right to appeal this decision and extend your hospital stay. Hospitals are required to furnish you with information on your hospital discharge appeal rights within two days of your admission and before you are discharged. Appeals may be submitted in writing or by phone, and they are reviewed immediately by the Quality Improvement Organization (QIO), a panel of doctors, and assorted other health care experts who contract with the federal government to ensure quality care for Medicare beneficiaries. You will only be responsible for applicable cost shares during the additional days of your hospital stay. The QIO will inform you and the hospital of its decision within one calendar day of receiving all applicable requested information.

Long-Term Care Ombudsman

There are long-term care ombudsman programs in every state. An ombudsman is a resident advocate who helps resolve problems between residents and facilities. Your local ombudsman can tell you whether complaints have been filed against the facilities you are considering, and advise you on how to obtain inspection reports, and how to evaluate that information, if you are considering a skilled nursing home. An ombudsman can counsel you with regard to specific residences, but may not be able to answer all of your questions due to legal reasons. If they encourage you to look elsewhere, take it under serious consideration.

Two of the primary functions of a long-term care ombudsman are to identify, investigate, and resolve resident complaints and to provide information and consultation to residents and their families. They can also help you by suggesting aging-in-place solutions and other aging services that you may be able to utilize in addition to senior housing.

To find your local ombudsman, check the "Senior Citizens' Services and Organizations" in the Yellow Pages or call the Eldercare Locator at 1-800-677-1116. For more information on long-term care ombudsman programs, read Chapter 14 and see the listing for the National Long Term Care Ombudsmen Resource Center in Appendix C.

Geriatric Care Managers

Geriatric care managers are the human equivalent of a one-stop shop. They can perform geriatric assessments, develop care plans, educate you on housing and service options that are tailored to your needs and budget, advocate for you, arrange services, give recommendations and referrals, coordinate care, and act as a liaison between the people and services involved in your care plan.

In addition, they are one of the most "plugged in" aging services professionals you could ask for. Local care managers are likely to have current or past clients in senior housing arrangements in your community, so not only are they likely to be very familiar with some of the residences you are considering, but they may also be able to provide you names of residents or family members who would might agree to speak to you directly about the facility and their personal experience there.

Geriatric care managers may have a background in social work, nursing, gerontology, public health, or other aging-related experience. Some care managers specialize in certain areas. Here are some questions you may consider asking:

- What are your areas of specialty?

- Are you a fiduciary?

- Can you advise me on Medicare and Medicaid issues?

- What is your educational experience?

- How long have you provided geriatric care management (GCM) services?

- Are you approved for Medicare reimbursement?

- Are you a member of the National Association of Professional Geriatric Care Managers (NAPGCM)?

As their businesses rely on referrals and word-of-mouth recommendations, ask for references before hiring a care manager. An effective, experienced care manager will have excellent references from grateful seniors and family members.

You can find geriatric care managers through the National Association of Professional Geriatric Care Managers by calling 520-881-8008 or visiting the website at www.caremanager.org.

Many geriatric care managers are in private practice. But you can also find care managers who work for community agencies and provide consultation and services for free or on a sliding scale.

Your Doctor

Your doctor can be a great source of information, especially because he is familiar with your medical history. The medical community comprises a network of health care professionals who regularly work together with shared patients or clients, and who regularly make referrals to other specialists. If your doctor isn't able to provide the information or advice that you need directly, he will be able to recommend other health and medical professionals who can help you. If your doctor is a gerontologist, then you are very fortunate. As established members of the aging services community, gerontologists have extra training in specialized areas that concern seniors and their health, and will be familiar with the options that are available locally.

Talk to your doctor as early on as possible about the process of looking for senior housing. Your doctor can help you determine what type of setting is the most appropriate fit for your needs.

Support Groups and Religious Groups

There are countless support groups for seniors and caregivers. Support groups may include any organized or informal group where you can seek information, support, and advice on choosing senior housing. Whether you prefer online forums or the more traditional in-person support group that meets regularly, seek out groups whose members have experience in what you are going through. Personal advice and even anecdotal information about one's personal experience in choosing senior housing can be invaluable in helping you make a decision. Members of a support network are usually happy to discuss conflicts and roadblocks in the decision-making process as well as suggesting potential solutions.

Members of your church, temple, synagogue, mosque, or other place of worship, including your pastor or rabbi, are another great resource you can turn to. Faith groups are built-in support networks that you can rely on when you are unsure of how to proceed. You are not the first person to be making a decision on senior housing. Let other seniors and families who have been down the path before you help guide you on your way.

Residents and Families

Who better to provide information and advice than current residents (and their families) of the residences on your shortlist? After all, no one is in a better position to tell you what it's like there. If you were at the beginning of your career or switching to another profession, you might consider setting up informational interviews with people who do what you want to do. This is like that: interview the people whose shoes you could potentially be in very soon.

Resident and family councils are a great place to start, and can give you a good idea of what to expect as a new resident and provide insight into daily life. You might try to coordinate a visit to coincide with a council meeting; if you do, arrange this with the facility in advance.

Besides coordinating with resident and family councils, you can also talk to these folks individually. In small groups or on a one-on-one basis, you may be able to get the most truthful and frank responses you are looking for. You might want to schedule a time when you know families will be visiting, such as a weekend day; that way you can talk to both.

Use the earlier chapters in this book as a guide for specific questions that you might consider asking. Here are examples:

- Are you happy with your accommodations? Why or why not?

- Do you like the food?

- Do you like the activities that are offered?

- Are you satisfied with the care? If not, why?

- Are you satisfied with the staff? Are they reliable and professional?

- Are you satisfied with the level of privacy? Do staff members knock on the door before entering your room or residence?

- If you could do it all over again, would you make the same choice to live here? If not, why?

- What are the things you like and dislike most about living here?

Ask whether they would like to share any additional information with you, such as any advice or tips on how to make your choice, and specific things they've learned from going through the process themselves. Don't forget: you want to know if they recommend the place. Do they? If it's not clear from their answers, ask that question directly. You may want to ask any questions of a sensitive nature, such as these, out of earshot of staff members so that the residents and families will not be self-conscious about answering truthfully.

Also be observant of residents when you visit. They could potentially be your neighbors. What are they doing on your visit? Is their activity level on par with yours? Are people participating in the activity if one occurs during your visit? Try to participate in an activity yourself if you are able. Is it enjoyable?

Facility Staff

When you talk to staff members, ask them how long they have worked at the residence. Long-term care facilities have notoriously high turnover rates. Just as longevity is a sign of stability in upper management, it is a sign of job satisfaction in other staff members, which can be a great thing for residents. High rates of turnover may not necessarily be a bad sign, but they could be an indicator of poor overall operation and performance; constant understaffing easily translates into overworked staff and unhappy residents and family members. In addition, the stress resulting from low pay, demanding work, and unsupportive management makes for an unhappy staff. Use your best judgment. It's usually pretty easy to tell if a person is truly happy in her job when you ask directly: do you like working here?

Also ask caregivers how many residents they care for. The fewer people, the better: it means more individualized care.

Other Resources That Can Help

There are many other agencies, organizations, websites, and publications you can turn to for help in sorting through senior housing options, including your local Area Agency on Aging, the Better Business Bureau, state licensing agencies, and accrediting agencies. For more information, see Appendixes B and C.

The "Senior Citizens' Services and Organizations" section in your local Yellow Pages provides information on dozens of senior and aging-related services, from transportation to referral services, adult protective services, your long-term care ombudsman, the department of aging and adult services, legal assistance hotlines for seniors, senior centers, and more.

The Eldercare Locator is an excellent service provided by the U.S. Administration on Aging. Call toll-free at 1-800-677-1116 or visit www.eldercare.gov to learn about senior housing and care resources in your community as well as federal resources. The Eldercare Locator can also provide you with the contact information for your local Area Agency on Aging.

If you are comparing nursing homes, two great sites to visit for more information include Medicare, which offers the Nursing Home Compare feature at www.Medicare.gov, and Consumer Reports, which maintains the Nursing Home Quality Monitor at www.consumerreports.org.

Nursing Home Compare is an online tool you can use to help you find and compare nursing homes that are certified for Medicare or Medicaid. You can search for the factors that are most important to you, such as location, type of ownership (e.g.., for-profit or nonprofit), number of beds, whether the facilities have a resident and/or family council, and much more. Nursing Home Compare offers detailed information on the most recent health inspections, staffing data, quality measures, and fire safety inspections.

Consumer Report's Nursing Home Quality Monitor is another online tool for comparing nursing homes. It is more user-friendly than Nursing Home Compare for several reasons. First, it provides more detailed and thorough explanations of individual nursing home performance, taking into account nursing home inspection reports and weighting the data to give individual homes a score you can use to compare performance as relative to other facilities. The Nursing Home Quality Monitor also divides nursing homes into two categories: "consider" and "avoid." However, we advocate using both Nursing Home Compare and the Nursing Home Quality Monitor as dual sources for background checking nursing homes. Together, the information from both sources will give you the most accurate picture.

There are many referral agencies, websites, and publications that provide free information on senior housing options to consumers. In most cases, the information in these venues is provided directly from the residences and is essentially marketing material that has been minimally edited by the referrer. In some instances, no editing or fact-checking has been done at all. Facilities either pay the referrer for a listing, or pay upon placement (meaning you move in). If you utilize a referral resource, make sure that you use it as a starting point only, to learn about the senior housing options in your area. Back it up with your own research.

If you have the luxury of time, then plan ahead and be thorough in your research. But if there is one thing we can stress, it is this: don't wait unnecessarily to make a decision. You don't want to be forced to make a decision when you are in crisis mode, such as after selling your house and having nowhere to go, or being in a position where you need care immediately and don't have a plan in place. A fall, accident, or other health crisis can occur at any time. Many residences have long waiting lists. If time is on your side, take advantage of it, and get your name on the waiting list at your first choice. If you are still having difficulty making up your mind, ask whether you can stay overnight or for a few days to try it on for size.

And remember: you always have the option of moving again if the senior housing residence you move to isn't a good fit. It shouldn't be the first course of action you consider before giving the place a real shot and giving it enough time for any wrinkles to be ironed out. Moving can also be disruptive and costly. However, if it truly is a poor fit and you are not happy there, it's better to move to a place that meets your needs on all levels.

So take the plunge. Don't allow yourself to be stymied by indecision. Good luck!

Chapter 12

Making the Transition

Making the transition from home to designated senior housing is a big change. For most of us, big changes cause at least a little discomfort—and sometimes a lot. No matter where you're moving from, one of the most difficult things about making this transition is the feeling of being removed from familiar surroundings, family, friends, and neighbors. Having to adjust to an entirely new environment and a new routine can be stressful for anyone.

Many things can prompt a move to senior housing. Chief among these are an increasing need for support services and care, a change in finances, and a sudden change in health status. New and prospective residents of assisted living facilities and nursing homes may face the added stress of having recently lost a spouse. Each of these reasons on their own can be extremely difficult to cope with; combined, they can be overwhelming. The emotional aspect of making this transition must not be overlooked. Feelings of fear, anger, helplessness, doubt, uncertainty, and depression are extremely common among seniors who are planning a move, or who have recently moved to senior housing. If a health event triggered the move, you may feel frustrated at your new limitations and scared about what the changes might mean for your future. All of this is not to say that everyone experiences these feelings, but many do.

One thing to keep in mind is that your new surroundings can also enrich your life immeasurably. The convenience of housing designed for senior living, the support services, the safety of living in a secure community, the opportunities to forge new friendships, the social opportunities—these are just a few of the many things that can help ease the difficulty of this transition and help you adjust to your new surroundings. And if you are moving to a long-term care facility, don't forget the basics: you will have access to the care you need, which is critical. While stressful events may have triggered your move, there are many positive aspects to moving to senior housing.

In this chapter, we'll discuss some of those positive aspects as well as ways to help you adjust to your new life, beginning with preparing for the move, to settling in to day-to-day life in your new environment.

Moving Out and Moving In

Plan ahead for the move if that is at all possible. The more time you have to prepare, the better. A rushed move is likely to exacerbate feelings of stress, fear, and doubt. Planning ahead will not only give you time to come to terms to this decision on an emotional level, but it will also grant you more control over the moving and packing process, and extra time to decide what things you want to take with you, which things to give away, and which things to put in storage. This alone will help a great deal.

Before you move into your new residence, compile a list of questions you and your family still need answers to. Perhaps you still have questions about facility policies, fees, payment and insurance coverage, or the move itself. Once you have all of these questions in hand, make an appointment with the admissions director, administrator, or other person in charge, to go over the list in person or over the phone.

Depending on the housing arrangement you select, the paperwork can be quite extensive. Fill this out as early as possible. It may answer some of your questions, particularly about facility policies and financial details. Make sure you understand the eligibility requirements for Medicare and Medicaid, if applicable, and if you have a long-term care insurance policy, find out the coverage details that apply to your new living arrangement if you don't already know. Make sure all costs are detailed, including what is covered in the basic rates and what is not. By now you should have a schedule of fees. If something is not on there, ask about it, and if necessary, have the appropriate person add that to the fee schedule and print out a new copy.

The facility may require a complete medical history. You can get this from your doctor. Request that it be sent to you directly so that you can check it for accuracy and add details as necessary. Then you can forward it to the facility.

You may also choose to share relevant personal information, such as habits, preferences, and pet peeves, when you meet with the admissions director. These things can help the staff get a general sense of who you are before you move in. They can be noted on your file, consulted in drafting your care or service plan, and/or used to match you with a compatible roommate. Obviously, you will need to make some adjustments to your daily routine once you move in, but it may be possible to continue doing many of the things you enjoy, without interruption, in your new home. What personal information you share with the staff is up to you, but the more you share, the better they will be able to help make this transition as comfortable and as seamless as possible.

Here are some examples of personal information you might consider sharing:

- What do you and don't you like to eat?

- If not already noted on your medical chart, do you have any dietary restrictions?

- Are you an early riser or a night owl?

- How is your vision? Does it get worse at night?

- If you have impaired vision or mobility, would you like staff to help you?

- If you require bathing assistance, do you prefer baths or showers?

- Have you had to share a room or bathroom in another senior housing arrangement?

- Do you have any concerns about having a roommate?

- If you are reading this book for a loved one, does he or she become confused or disoriented in new surroundings? Does it become worse at night?

- Is religion important to you? Is attending religious services important to you? Would you like a clergy member to visit you once you move in?

- Do you smoke or drink? Do you have a preference as to whether your roommate smokes or drinks? (Some senior housing arrangements are nonsmoking facilities; others that allow smoking have policies regarding where smoking is allowed. You can request a nonsmoking roommate if you have a preference.)

- What are your hobbies or favorite pastimes? Do you have any special interests? Do you have a routine, such as reading the morning newspaper with breakfast or going for a walk after supper?

- Do you enjoy socializing in groups?

The day you move in is a big day and you are likely to be nervous. If you haven't already enlisted family and friends to help you on moving day, do so now. Extra hands are always useful during a move! And having friendly, familiar faces around will help you relax and become acclimated to your new environment and ensure that you won't be completely out of your personal comfort zone. Ask those who will be with you on that day if they would like to stay for a meal or an activity after unpacking your belongings or even during a break.

Facility Guidelines

Before moving in, the facility will discuss moving guidelines with you, and your family, if appropriate. This includes things such as what to bring and what is not allowed. For example, if you plan to bring your own furnishings, they may require prior approval to ensure that they are safe (e.g., fireproof) and practical for the living space. If you would like to bring your pet, ask the facility about its pet policy beforehand. There may also be general guidelines regarding the day of your move. Check with the facility well in advance of your move date.

Help With Moving

If you are moving from the home where you have lived for many years, it can be extremely difficult to pack up all of your belongings, much less decide where they should go. The process of packing, moving, and getting rid of belongings accumulated over a lifetime can be daunting and emotional. Unearthing and handling items that you haven't seen for a very long time inevitably brings up memories associated with them, whether it's a keepsake from your first date with your husband, or an heirloom tea set that has been in your family for generations. You may feel an obligation to keep certain things, especially if they were a gift from someone special, or to keep certain items in the family if they have been passed down to you. But you must also be practical. This is where others can help. If you have the luxury of planning ahead for your move, family and friends can be an invaluable resource when it comes to sorting, organizing, and making decisions about where your belongings should go. But in the likely event that your moving needs will be too great to depend solely on help from family, you will need to hire professional movers.

There are countless moving companies to choose from. But did you know that there is a segment of professional movers who specialize in working with seniors? The National Association of Senior Move Managers (NASMM) is the only national nonprofit organization that works exclusively with older adults. They are very familiar with the sensitive issues associated with downsizing and transitioning to senior housing at this stage of life. Not only can they provide excellent advice based on long-established experience, but these movers provide an empathetic ear while doing so. The NASMM referral network lists senior move managers in 46 states. For more information, contact the NASMM at www.nasmm.com or toll-free at 1-877-606-2766. Alternatively, you can check the listings in your local Yellow Pages under "Movers" and "Moving Services."

Storage Facilities

Downsizing is common when moving from home to any senior housing arrangement, as well as moving between senior housing types, such as from independent living to assisted living. If there is not sufficient storage space for your belongings in your new residence but there are certain items that you just don't want to part with, you may have to put them in storage. Here are some tips to keep in mind when selecting a storage facility:

- Visit in person. If you can't do it yourself, send a family member or a trusted friend to do it for you. Check the storage units to make sure they are clean, dry, free of odors, with enough room for your belongings. Check with the Better Business Bureau (www.bbb.org) and the Bureau of Consumer Protection (www.ftc.gov/bcp) and ask whether any complaints have been filed in the past.

- Find out about insurance. Long-term storage facilities often offer insurance to protect your belongings from accidents, damage, and theft. Not all companies offer insurance. If you have homeowner's or renter's insurance, you may be able to pay a premium so that your belongings may be covered while in storage; this could be cheaper than obtaining a new, separate policy. It is prudent to get insurance, as storage facility agreements usually free the company from being responsible for damage or loss that occurs while your items are in storage. If you take out insurance, you will be required to provide an inventory of all items to be covered. Also make sure that the policy can be changed, if necessary, in the future. This is essential if you plan to add or remove items from storage that are on the inventory.

- Ask about security features. Storage facilities may employ security guards, motion detectors, video surveillance, alarms, or a combination of these features. Make sure you are comfortable with the level of security that is offered.

- If any of your belongings are sensitive to heat or cold, choose a facility that offers units with climate control.

- Ask about fees and hours of access. Storage facility fees are fairly straightforward at most places. The one thing to watch out for is late fees. Ask how much they are and when they are charged (i.e., is there a grace period?).

Getting Rid of Your Things

If you are making a move to senior housing and expect that it will be permanent, then you will probably need to get rid of most things in your home rather than put them in storage. You can either give them away or sell them. Are there any items you want to keep in your family? Make a list of those items, and note to whom you would like to give them. You can also donate items to charitable organizations like Goodwill and the Salvation Army, which accept donations of clothing, jewelry, furniture, assorted household goods, sporting equipment, books, electronics, and more. See Appendix C for information, and how you can make a tax-deductible donation to either of these two organizations.

Estate sales for seniors who are moving from their longtime homes are very common. Selling the items in your home through an estate sale is a relatively fast and convenient way to empty your home of belongings that you will not be able to bring with you to your new home. It can also be a great way to raise cash that you can use to help finance your move. You can either hold the sale yourself or hire a professional estate sale company or specialist to hold it for you. Planning and holding an estate sale yourself is a lot of work, so if you have a lot of items to sell, you may want to consider hiring a professional to help you—it will save you a considerable amount of time and effort, and is likely to get better results than if you were to hold the sale yourself.

Here is how it works. Professional estate sale companies usually charge a percentage of the proceeds from the sale (on average, ranging between 20 and 50 percent), so you won't have to pay until afterward. In addition, professional estate sale companies have proven avenues of advertising sales and often have a loyal following, which means that your chances of having more people interested in your sale—and ultimately of selling more items—may be better than if you were to manage the sale on your own. The most common advice that all estate sale professionals give their clients is this: do not throw anything away! A specialist will inventory and tag (set a price on) every item to be sold and will be able to identify items of value that might surprise you. Old posters, magazines, postcards, and toys that seem like junk can be very valuable. The real "junk" left over at the end of the sale can be donated.

If you hire an estate sale company, make sure you understand what the payment terms are before you commit. Also ask about their advertising practices. An experienced estate sale company will use a variety of advertising methods, which may include a combination of the following: classified ads in the local newspaper(s); signage in your neighborhood (to be removed promptly after the sale); flyers or handbills detailing the items for sale, to be distributed to antique shops, antique malls, and flea markets; e-mail advertising to interested individuals who have opted to be contacted about estate sales; and other proven techniques. The most effective advertising of estate sales combines multiple methods for optimal results. To find an estate sale specialist or company in your area, check your local Yellow Pages under "Estates—Sales, Appraisal & Liquidation."

What to Bring

Think about the items you would like to bring with you to your new residence. Personal items can help you feel more at home in your new surroundings. Most residences, even nursing homes, will allow you to bring small pieces of furniture to personalize your room or apartment. Things such as a TV, radio, photographs, artwork, and books can go a long way toward making your space more comfortable.

If your space is limited and you are an avid reader, take an inventory of your books and bring this list with you when you move. Then coordinate with your family to bring new books with them when they visit and bring the titles you have read back with them when they leave. Many senior housing residences take part in a visiting library program as well.

If you wish to bring jewelry or other valuables with you and are concerned about keeping them safe, you should consult with the staff to see whether there are secure storage options. Of course, if you live in a private apartment, this may not be an issue. However, in nursing homes and other shared living spaces, there is the possibility of damage or loss. Keep this in mind when you decide what you would like to take with you to your new home. You might also consider purchasing a small safe or locked trunk (make sure there is room first).

A note about cash: you may need to keep some cash on hand for groceries, meals out, beauty salon appointments, and the like. If you are not comfortable keeping the cash in your room or apartment, the facility may already have a system in place for residents' personal accounts. If your expenses are in-house, then it's likely they can just be put on a tab that is deducted from your personal account.

If someone other than yourself will be doing your laundry, you may wish to have labels sewn into your clothing in case of a mix-up.

Help from Family

Your family can help you adjust to your new home in many ways. Visiting is one of the obvious and very vital ways that your family can help ease your transition. But there are many other ways they can pitch in.

One way is to ask your family if they would be interested in joining the facility's family council. Most assisted living facilities, nursing homes, and CCRCs have family councils, but if one does not exist, you can always suggest starting one. Family councils function slightly differently from place to place, but all of them share the two primary goals of advocacy and involvement.

On a facility level, family councils can organize, sponsor, or support events; they can help new residents and families adjust to life at the facility; and they often function as a support network for families. Family councils are useful because they can influence the decisions and policies that are made at the facility, which will affect you, as a resident. Family councils may have a structured meeting place and time, and specific objectives, or not. They give families an opportunity to discuss issues and concerns regarding the facility.

Family councils can be very influential in enacting change. Facilities are likely to respond to concerns presented by the group and are generally willing to work together toward a resolution whenever possible. Joining a family council is a great way for your family to remain involved in your life, keep up on the goings-on where you live, and build a network with family members of other residents.

Another opportunity for family to be involved is to volunteer. Many senior housing residences, particularly those that are community-oriented, welcome volunteers. You can have your relative(s) call the administrator to ask whether they have specific needs; or if your family member has a particular idea in mind, then by all means, have him call and ask whether it would be okay! The activity director is another good person to connect with for volunteering opportunities. From joining a group outing to giving art lessons to helping out in the garden, there are all kinds of ways your family member can be a helpful presence in your new home.

Settling In

It's more than likely that your new home probably won't feel like home for a while. That's okay. We will share some tried-and-true steps you can take that will help you get there. All you need to do is keep putting one foot in front of the other.

The First Few Weeks

No big surprise here: the first few weeks will probably require the most effort on your part. It is not simply a move. This is the beginning of a significant life change. If you're like most of us, you'll probably never forget how you felt on the first day of school, or transferring in as a new student, or walking into the office on your first day at a new job. Those situations are rife with expectation and anxiety about how you will fit in, how others will like you, and whether you will like it yourself. These first few weeks are like that. So get ready to settle in, meet your new neighbors, and experience the community's culture firsthand.

Getting Used to Rules and New Routines

As much as we'd all like to think we can roll with the punches, the truth is, most of us are used to things being a certain way and that's how we like them. If you've lived under your own roof for years, then getting used to the differences in your new living arrangement can be tough. Speaking of living under one roof, if you have children, you've probably said at one point or another, "While you're under my roof, you'll abide by my rules!" Well, guess what? It's your turn to abide by someone else's rules.

Make sure you understand the rules and policies before you move in, and if you have questions, ask. About half of getting used to new rules is about setting expectations. If you know what is expected of you, then you can act accordingly, and you won't be surprised when a rule is enforced. The other half? That involves time and patience.

The same idea applies to learning to adapt to new routines. If you are living in a private residence, you'll have more control over your personal schedule than if you are sharing a room with another resident. Be ready to make some changes, but also know that facility staff will try to work with you whenever possible to ensure that you are comfortable and that reasonable requests are met.

Getting to Know Staff Members

Don't be bashful in getting to know staff members and asking for their help when you need it. If you are worried about being a bother, don't be. The staff is there to help you adjust and to provide support when it is needed. In fact, they will probably be making an effort to get to know you, inviting you to participate in planned activities, or offering to introduce you to fellow residents. Take them up on these invitations if you are feeling up to it, or let them know that another time might be better, but that you appreciate the thought. Staff members of senior housing have seen it all, so don't be shy if you are feeling sad or out of place. In fact, many communities employ social workers whom you can talk to about these feelings.

When your family and friends come to visit, give them a tour of your new home if they haven't seen it yet, and introduce them to staff members as you walk through. It will be nice for both sides to meet and put a face to the name of the people they've been hearing about in conversations with you.

Getting to know the staff is the same as getting to know anybody else. Ask them about their families, what they like to do, where they're from. Simple questions like these can pave the way to an open dialogue and a good relationship. If they do something nice for you, thank them. Everyone appreciates good manners and being recognized for their kindness or a job well done, and staff is no different. Also, learn staff members' roles so you know who you can go to if you have a problem.

One thing that can be hard is having new caregivers. If you had caregivers at your previous residence, it can be an emotional process to get used to a new person helping you. The same is true if you have never had a caregiver before; not only do you have to get used to the new person, but it may feel as though you have lost a certain measure of independence. Just remember that you are not the first person to experience these frustrations. Be honest with yourself about how you feel, and if you are comfortable sharing those feelings with your caregiver, we encourage you to do so. We think you'll find that they are very understanding.

Getting to Know the Area

If you live in independent or assisted living, explore your neighborhood. Go for a walk or a drive. It can be fun to get to know the area and you may spot a coffee shop, beauty salon, bookstore, shopping center, or other points of interest for future outings.

Do you know what kinds of amenities are available in the neighborhood? If not, you can ask the administrator for ideas. Or if you are ready to make friends, ask other residents. They can tell you which post office branch stays open the latest, which movie theater has a cheaper matinee, and which restaurants have senior specials. Perhaps you can surprise your family during their next visit by already having an idea of where you'd like to go when they take you out.

Overcoming Loss and Getting to Know Your Neighbors

Without a doubt, one of the hardest things about aging is losing the people closest to us. For people who haven't experienced it, it's hard for them to fathom what it's like to lose a spouse, or a dear friend whom you have known for decades. It's easy to withdraw and isolate yourself so that you don't feel the need to explain why you are sad, angry, or frustrated.

There are all kinds of circumstances that can trigger a move to senior housing. Sure, for some the move may seem like no big deal; perhaps they are very social people by nature, or very adaptable, or just really wanted to move out of their family home, which had become too much trouble to look after. But for many others, this is a difficult transition, too. Perhaps they have suffered a health event that recently changed their life, or lost a spouse, or went through a divorce or other event that limited their assets and forced them to downsize.

The point is that this transition is not easy for most people. But you don't have to go through it alone. It's hard to talk about matters that are personal and private. You don't have to do that unless you want to. But if you can, try to view this transition as an opportunity to make new friends. This in itself can be extremely rewarding.

Make small goals, such as talking to one new person each day. Gradually, you will come to know your neighbors, and they will get to know you.

Participating in Planned Activities

If the community has an activity calendar, take advantage of planned activities. You'll be meeting so many new people in a very short period. Participating in activities will help you connect names and faces and help you get to know staff and fellow residents. Activities are also a great way to take your mind off your concerns, even if it's only temporary. You are allowed to have fun. Let yourself!

Make sure planned activities occur if they are on the activity calendar. If the schedule is not up to date, request an updated copy. Feel free to talk to the activity director to suggest activities to add to the calendar. She is likely to appreciate your input; it can be hard to create activities for other people, so when residents suggest activities, the suggestions are usually welcomed, provided they are practical!

Resuming Favorite Pastimes

It's important to stay engaged and nurture your interests even if your abilities decline. Engaging your mind and cultivating an interest in things outside of yourself and your daily environment is natural and healthy at every age. Don't let favorite pastimes fall by the wayside simply because your residence has changed.

If you have always loved to garden, see if you can continue this hobby at your new residence. Many senior housing facilities welcome resident gardeners and may even have raised planters and stools so that you can enjoy yourself without worrying about "overdoing" it. If there isn't a garden, perhaps you could get permission to start one with some help. Indoor gardens or window-box gardens may be allowed if this isn't possible.

Perhaps you have always felt it important to give back or engage in social services. If that is the case, perhaps you can volunteer in your community or tutor a student. Or perhaps you are an avid reader and would be interested in joining a book club or arranging for regular outings to the public library. Do it!

Keeping in Touch

Keeping in touch with loved ones can really help you through this transition period. During the first two weeks, try to have a familiar face drop by to see you at least twice. As time progresses, you may decide to keep this as a weekly ritual, or come up with another schedule. There are a number of ways to keep in touch—visits, phone calls, e-mail, letters—all of which will help you remain connected to the people you love. Don't underestimate the power of remaining in touch with the outside world. Your family and friends can reassure you and support you through the early stages of this transition, which are usually the most emotionally challenging.

If you don't have a private apartment with access to your own phone, get a calling card. Minutes can easily be refilled by using a credit card, accessing your personal account at the facility, or having a family member do this for you. It's reassuring that you will only be a phone call away from loved ones if you have a bad day and need to hear a friendly voice, or to call and wish your grandson a happy birthday, or simply to chat with friends and family.

Who doesn't love getting a personal letter or care package in the mail? Whether you're 5 or 85, that doesn't change. If your loved ones are unable to visit often due to distance, schedules, or other reasons, encourage them to keep in touch via good old-fashioned correspondence.

Ask them to send photos of special family events that you cannot attend or let them know how much you enjoy getting postcards when they travel so you can see where they've been. If you can't get together for special occasions and holidays, be sure to exchange cards. Long letters are nice, but even a short note can brighten your day (and theirs!). Get in the habit of dropping notes in the mail to keep in touch with family and friends and let them know that you are thinking of them. Your mailbox will be full in no time.

If you enjoy keeping up on news and current events, and if there are any topics of particular interest, such as local politics, or health news, ask your family members to send clippings of these items or bring them when they visit. If it's a shared interest, it will give you something to talk about when your loved ones visit. Or you can read them on your own later.

Correspondence is also a great way to renew relationships after a prolonged absence. If you have fallen out of touch with a friend or relative and you miss that person, send a short note to let her know that you have been thinking of her and that you would like to get back in touch. Chances are, you have been in her thoughts as well.

Visits From Family and Friends

Regular visits from family and friends are so important. They will help you feel connected to your life outside your senior housing community, and it will help maintain relationships that are just as important to your loved ones as they are to you.

One thing you should be prepared for is this: just as it may be hard for you to adjust to living in a senior housing facility, it may be equally as hard for your family, who may have some anxiety or find it emotionally difficult to see you in such an environment at first. If you have relocated to a nursing home, your family may feel uncomfortable in these initial visits because they are not used to seeing you in a health care facility. Perhaps other residents who have greater limitations make them scared that this will happen to you, too. They may think that it is like visiting you in the hospital. It's likely that your visitors may find the setting depressing but are too embarrassed to say anything to you because they don't want to offend you. You can help them through all of these feelings.

One way of doing so is to gently remind them that we all grow older and face health issues that cannot be helped. It's a fact of life, and it doesn't have to be sad. If you have lived a full life, have people who love you to visit you, and are receiving quality health care, then you have many things to be thankful for. Remind your visitors of this, and remind them that you enjoy their company very much.

If possible, ask your loved ones to plan visits with you in advance. That way you will be able to look forward to the visit and be ready to accept visitors. Oftentimes visitors say that they will just "drop in." This can be inconvenient if you are involved in another activity when they arrive, or you are tired, or are not feeling up to visitors. Also, life is busy. Sometimes things come up, and without a specific time pre-arranged the visit is put on hold—sometimes indefinitely. Planning ahead and setting a specific time for the visit can help make it enjoyable for both of you, and ease feelings of anger and guilt if a promised visit doesn't occur.

For reasons we've already mentioned, sometimes visits in your new home can be awkward. They shouldn't be. Sometimes resuming favorite activities that you have always enjoyed together can help ease your way back into comfortably spending time together and enjoying each other's company in this new environment. Whether it's playing cards, reading newspapers together and discussing current events, or simply chatting about news of your old neighborhood, pick up where you left off. If you don't have a deck of cards, a cribbage board, or a backgammon set (or fill in your favorite game here), then ask your guest to bring it along on the visit. Or ask the activity director if these items are on hand for you to borrow.

What's nice about visits is that they keep you connected to the outside world. Don't be shy. Ask your visitors to bring a little bit of the outside in with them. Help them by making specific requests. For example, if your visitor has a pet that you have always loved, ask if the pet can come by for a visit. Attention-loving pets are usually spoiled by pet-loving residents, so as long as pet visits are allowed, have your visitor bring along Fido or Whiskers next time. This can make for a very social visit, the animal will relish the attention, and other residents are usually delighted. You can also go for a walk together when your visitor arrives.

Ask your family to bring favorite treats from home, something you can't get in the facility. If you have your own apartment with a kitchen or kitchenette, this shouldn't be a problem. But if you are in a shared situation such as a nursing home, the facility may have rules about storing food that won't be consumed right away. Make sure your family knows about these rules.

Visitors can also bring photos and videos of important family occasions that you cannot attend, such as your grandchildren's birthday parties, sporting events or graduation ceremonies, or a special anniversary party. This is yet another way to stay connected to loved ones in the outside world.

If you have a hard time writing letters, ask your visitor for help. They will probably be happy to write the letters for you if you dictate them. If it's a nice day, go outside and write letters in the sunshine!

Have your family join you for a meal at your new residence, or go with them to a restaurant. If there's somewhere you'd like to go, let them know. They will probably welcome your interest and will be happy that they can take you someplace that you want to go. If you are not able to leave the facility, you may be able to reserve a private dining area or dining room where you can have privacy when your family comes to share a meal with you. Most facilities have this and will be happy to accommodate you as long as you make the request in advance.

Asking the facility administrator about conjugal visits is a sensitive subject, one most new and prospective residents are not comfortable bringing up. So here is what you need to know: your new home is your *home*, which means that your partner should be welcome, and you have every right to continue this fundamental aspect of nurturing your relationship after you live separately. The Residents' Bill of Rights, which is required at Medicare and Medicaid-certified facilities, protect this right. You have the right to private conjugal visits with your partner without intrusion from staff, unless your doctor deems this hazardous to your health. If you share a room with another resident, the facility should make arrangements for you and your spouse to ensure privacy. If you have a private apartment, this should not be an issue.

If you are able to go on outings when your family visits, by all means do so! Think about things you'd like to do. Perhaps you'd like to do a little shopping, or go out for a meal, or run some errands. These are all perfectly acceptable activities. It can be nice to get out and about, and your family will appreciate being able to help in this way. If you are up for it, let your family know that you would like to plan occasional outings with them on Sundays, to go to your neighborhood services, and then out for brunch, for example. Special occasions such as holidays, birthdays, and anniversaries may warrant an overnight stay.

Extended visits are usually encouraged as long as your health permits it. These could range from an afternoon outing to a weeklong vacation with family. Extended visits can do wonders for renewing your vigor and staying connected to loved ones at home, who you may no longer see very often. If you are in a long-term care facility, you may have to plan overnight or extended stays in advance with the facility administrator.

Communicating With Family

Another unfortunate but common side effect of moving to senior housing is that it can make conversations with family difficult. Understand that it is very likely that your loved ones are also experiencing a rush of emotions over your move to senior housing. It is very common for families to feel guilty and inadequate at not being able to care for you or provide a home as you have done for them. New residents often feel helpless over their situations because they are unsure of how they will adjust to life at the facility, whether they will like it and make friends, whether the care will be adequate, and, if a health event triggered their move, whether they will recover.

There is no use dwelling on these feelings, but it does help to be aware of them and address them. If you don't speak your mind, your family won't know how you're feeling, and vice versa. If you are angry or frustrated about your situation, it's okay to talk about it. Sometimes new residents have a tendency to put on a brave face when they talk to loved ones on the phone or when their families come to visit. Similarly, families sometimes feel the need to avoid talking about things that could make you, or them, uncomfortable. Both of you should talk about your concerns frankly. Working through these issues can help you and your family stay close and perhaps even develop stronger bonds.

If your family tries to change the subject, ask them to please be patient with you and allow you to express your feelings. Say that you would like to include them in what is going on in your life. You may have to reiterate this several times. It can be frustrating if your family members simply propose solutions or don't listen to you, so repeat your wish to talk about your feelings. Ultimately, this will help you both.

Perhaps the most significant thing you all can do to prevent the move from negatively impacting your relationship is to acknowledge the fact that certain external factors have changed, but that you still love and care for each other as you always have, and that you will continue to be there for each other as you can. Allow yourself to count on each other.

Reassure your family that your relationship with them does not have to change because your address did. Let them know that they can still turn to you. Even if you are physically disabled and have severe physical limitations, you can offer your love, support, humor, advice, and an empathetic ear when it is needed. Those things are invaluable. In turn, your family can provide love, support, and positive motivation. If they do not, gently remind them that you need these things.

All of you are likely to have frustrations over your move to senior housing. That is normal. Sometimes there is no easy resolution. That is normal, too. If you talk about it, it can be therapeutic. It helps to be able to vent your frustrations even when there is no clear solution, as long as you know that someone who cares about you hears what you are saying. Sometimes all you need is a sympathetic ear. You can request that if your family insists on "solving the problems."

Neglect or Abuse

If you are reading this book on behalf of a loved one, be sure to watch for signs of neglect or abuse. In some instances where substandard care is an issue, neglect is tantamount to abuse. Many of today's seniors grew up in an era where you put up with problems and didn't complain. Old habits die hard. Lots of seniors keep problems to themselves because they don't want to get anyone in trouble (like their caregivers) or burden anyone (like you or other family members), or because they are scared of possible retaliation if they report a problem. So it is up to you to be vigilant about checking in with your loved one regularly. Ask your loved one if she is experiencing any problems that you can help with, rather than simply asking if everything is okay. Leading the conversation this way can make it easier for her to open up to you.

Indicators of trouble will vary from person to person, but investigate if you notice significant changes in your loved one's mood, unexplained weight loss or gain, or other health issues that seem out of the ordinary. Read Chapter 14 for more information on resolving problems, including how to report a case of neglect or abuse.

Give It a Chance

The biggest key to any adjustment is patience. Give your new living situation a real chance and give yourself time to resolve any frustrations or concerns you may have about your living arrangements. Your family and friends can be a big help in supporting you during this transition period, and so can staff and fellow residents. One of the best aspects about moving to senior housing is being surrounded by peers who understand what it's like to be in your shoes. Open your heart to new possibilities and new friendships. We hope that your new living arrangement is a success.

Chapter 13

Working With Staff and Caregivers

In most senior housing arrangements, even if you do not require daily care, you will interact with staff members on a daily basis. The staff works as a team, with some members performing behind the scenes and others taking center stage. From preparing and serving meals to organizing and leading activities, reevaluating your care or service plan, providing support during a period of transition, and providing essential health care services, there are a variety of ways in which you will rely on the staff.

The relationships you develop with the staff, especially the people who you interact with on a day-to-day basis, are very important, and can affect your experience as a resident significantly. As senior housing providers the staff is responsible for providing a safe living environment, and as long-term care professionals they must provide quality health care as it is needed. But you have a responsibility, too. It is up to you to communicate your needs and preferences so that the staff can do their jobs well and effectively, and ensure that you are satisfied with your care and your living environment.

To do that, it is important to recognize the value in establishing a foundation of respect and trust upon which you can build a relationship. We do not mean to suggest that you need to make friends with every staff member you come across if that is not something that interests you. If a relationship you develop with a staff member begets a bond, or blossoms into a friendship, it can be a wonderful and unexpected result. However, it is not the focus.

This chapter is your roadmap for learning how to work effectively with staff and caregivers, and it offers basic checkpoints along the way. We encourage you to review the route as you embark on your journey, but know that you will find your own path and wind up at a destination that is uniquely your own.

Establishing Positive Relationships

Positive relationships take work. Among other things, they require patience, understanding, and time. These are the building blocks you will use to establish a foundation of mutual trust and respect. In addition, consider the following guidelines for working effectively with staff and caregivers:

- **Communication.** The number-one key in establishing a positive relationship with staff or caregivers is good communication. Be open and honest about what you do and do not want. Communicate your preferences. Be patient if everything is not what you expected as soon as you move in. It may take some time to get there.

- **Reciprocity.** Good relationships are reciprocal; know that to some degree your actions influence the actions of others. If you treat a caregiver like a worker, you may be treated like "work." If you treat the caregiver like a person, expect to be treated as a person.

- **Consideration.** Be pleasant and considerate of staff and caregivers. Introduce them to your visitors. Say hello when you pass them in the hall or dining room. Talk to them about things other than your care. These informal types of interactions will help you establish trust, get to know one another naturally, and build on your relationship.

- **Appreciation.** Express your gratitude. Just as you should speak up if there is a problem, acknowledge a job well done by letting caregivers and staff know that you appreciate what they do for you.

Dealing With Frustration

The job of a caregiver is notoriously challenging. They are charged with taking care of elderly, ailing people who sometimes get worse no matter how well they do their job. Caregivers and administrators are under pressure to provide positive patient outcomes, which, frankly, is not always possible. On top of being asked to do a job that sometimes cannot be done, caregivers in long-term care facilities frequently face the added challenge of a heavy workload.

In addition to these challenges, caregivers are often underappreciated by residents and families who are unhappy with their care or perceived lack of progress, and who take out their frustrations on the caregiver. Regardless of whether these frustrations are warranted or not, verbally or physically abusing a staff member or caregiver is never okay. This includes making threats to the person (e.g., saying that you will report them) in an attempt to achieve a desired result (e.g., spending more time on your care). It is understandable to be frustrated, upset, concerned, and angry in light of health issues and complications. The same is true if you feel that the care you are receiving is substandard or lacking, or if the caregiver is simply not doing his job. However, there are proper channels for reporting a problem. Follow these channels for a resolution.

As a paying customer, you have the right to clean, safe housing and quality health care and support services as specified in your contract. As a resident, you are responsible for acting decorously. Caregivers are people, too. Even if you don't mean it, and are just saying things in the heat of the moment, the caregiver might not know that. Caregivers can feel unhappy and even unsafe when they are threatened. Caregivers and staff have rights to protect them, too. If a family member abuses a staff member, she could be banned from the facility.

Working With Facility Staff

In every long-term care facility, there is a chain of command. This hierarchy is necessary to ensure smooth daily operation, effective administration of care and services, and, ultimately, optimal resident satisfaction. The cardinal rule in working with facility staff is respecting the chain of command.

Every person working at the facility plays an essential role, and as a team they rely on one another to take care of their duties so that no one department or person becomes overwhelmed. Caregivers typically report to a charge (supervisory) nurse, who reports to the director of nursing, who reports to the administrator. Depending on your housing arrangement, there may be fewer or more links in this chain.

It is very important to understand the roles of the staff and caregivers you work with so you know who to talk to about a particular issue. For example, most issues regarding caregiving can be brought up with the caregiver or charge nurse. In special or very urgent cases, it may be appropriate to go to the director of nursing. Ask if you are not sure who to talk to about your issue. Try to respect the chain of command and avoid going over people's heads unless it is absolutely necessary and you have exhausted the usual routes of communication.

One of the great things about working with caregivers and staff in a senior housing arrangement is that there is a network of knowledgeable and experienced staff members who will be plugged into your "big picture," which includes information from your assessment and care plan (or service plan, as it is sometimes referred to in assisted living). You are welcome—and encouraged!—to get involved in drafting your care or service plan. This is a wonderful opportunity to work with staff and to communicate your needs and preferences. You can get involved before you move in or afterward, as your plan will be updated periodically. Family members can also take part in developing your plan. Write down any questions or concerns you have, as well as changes (if you will be reassessing a plan that is already in place) and goals you would like to discuss. Go over these points in the meeting, and be sure to follow up afterward if your expectations are not being met.

Facility Administrators

The role of the facility administrator varies from CCRCs to assisted living facilities to nursing homes, and varies by each individual residential arrangement. At a CCRC, it's typical to have multiple administrators for the various residential components, with a chain of command that reports to an executive director.

The job of an administrator is complex, multifaceted, and demanding. In general, administrators are responsible for planning and directing the day-to-day operations of a facility, supervising medical and nursing administration and personnel, supervising financial and marketing personnel, ensuring a high level of quality resident care and services, achieving and maintaining maximum rentals, attaining and maintaining a high degree of resident satisfaction, and ensuring the facility's compliance with federal and state regulations. As you can imagine, there are many tasks associated with each of these areas of the job. Administrators are busy individuals who are in charge of many things.

In working with a facility administrator, respect that person's time. In return, he will give you the respect of listening to you and helping you solve a problem when his assistance is necessary. After all, you wouldn't call the President if something was wrong with your breakfast, would you?

Caregivers and Nurses

In a long-term care living situation, your direct caregivers are likely to be certified nurse's aides (CNAs), who are sometimes referred to as certified nursing assistants. CNAs provide routine care and assistance with the activities of daily living (custodial care), and they are supervised by a licensed nurse. CNAs work very closely with residents and provide hands-on care, so they are often called "direct caregivers."

Because there are limits to the kinds of care that CNAs can provide, you will also work with the licensed nurse, who is able to provide skilled care that CNAs cannot, such as administering medication and performing treatments. A licensed nurse may be an RN (registered nurse), LPN (licensed practical nurse), or LVN (licensed vocational nurse).

If you have ever had a caregiver before, then you know that it takes some getting used to. Having another person care for you is a very intimate experience. Whether you are adjusting to a new caregiver or it is your first time, it can be both a challenging and emotional experience. It's not easy to be dependent on someone you don't know.

If you have a complaint about your care, bring it up with your caregiver or nurse to see whether there is a simple solution that you can come up with together. Try to use positive statements that begin with "I wish" or "I prefer" and politely explain what it is you'd like your caregiver to do differently. A gentle request is more likely to be honored than a cranky demand, and a caregiver who feels she is being accused of wrongdoing may not be as responsive as you would like. If the issue is not resolved by talking to the person directly, or if it is serious, consider working your way up the chain of command.

Working With Private Caregivers

Private caregivers, also known as private-hire caregivers, are simply caregivers who you hire on your own. Private caregivers assist seniors in all types of different environments, from private homes, to senior apartments and alternative independent living arrangements, assisted living residences, and nursing homes. If you live in a senior housing arrangement and not your own home, then you will need to make sure that private caregivers are allowed to work on premises. Check with the administrator or manager of your residence as well as the caregiver (if an independent contractor) or that person's agency.

Even though assisted living and skilled nursing both provide long-term care services, some residents eventually require more care than the facility is able to provide. After all, there are only so many employees to care for residents, and so many hours in the day. In light of increased needs and limited in-house resources, it is relatively common for residents in long-term care living situations to hire private caregivers to supplement the care they are already receiving. Private caregivers are also a big help for residents of independent living who are not quite ready to move to a long-term care facility. Whatever your case may be, you do have the option of hiring a private caregiver to help you stay in your current home.

Home Care and Home Health Care

No matter where you live, there are essentially two types of professional care that you can hire for help at home: home care and home health care. In Chapter 1, we explained custodial (nonmedical) care and skilled nursing care and discussed the differences between the two. The concepts are the same here: home care is considered custodial care, and home health care is skilled nursing care that is provided in a residential setting.

Home care is also called in-home care. It does not require a doctor's order; anyone who needs help may arrange for it on his own. Home care aides are professionally trained caregivers who, in addition to custodial care, may provide basic support services such as transportation to scheduled appointments, shopping and errands, light housekeeping and chores such as preparing meals, taking care of pets, and watering the plants. Caregivers can also assist with general household duties that you authorize them to, such as checking your mail, receiving deliveries, and helping you pay the bills. One of the most recognized benefits of home care, aside from the duties they perform, is companionship.

Home health care is also known as private duty nursing. Specialized services such as physical, occupational, and speech therapies may be incorporated as needed. The care is provided by a licensed nurse, who may be a RN, LPN, or LVN. These care providers sometimes work with trained home health aides who provide custodial care, assisting clients with the activities of daily living.

In this team framework, the home health aide and nurse operate in similar functions as a caregiver and nurse in a long-term care facility. Home health aides may administer medication to the senior, under a nurse's supervision.

Unlike home care, home health care requires a doctor's prescription. When your doctor prescribes home health care, you will also receive recommendations on where to go to get it, as most doctors and hospitals have established relationships with at least a few home health care agencies. That doesn't mean you have to follow the recommendation. You can also find home health care on your own.

Home health care agencies are licensed by the state and must adhere to federal regulations. To find and compare home health agencies, use the Home Health Compare feature on www.Medicare.gov.

When to Bring in Outside Help

When should you hire home care or home health care? There is no single right answer to this question. The easy answer is "when you need it." But there are dozens of reasons that may make sense for one person but won't apply to you, and vice versa. Every person's circumstances and reasons for bringing in outside help will be unique.

Home care and home health care can be used on an ongoing basis to help delay a move, prevent early institutionalization, or simply help prolong your independence if you don't require care but could use some assistance around the house. These services can also be used temporarily for a variety of reasons, such as helping you recover after a hospital stay, illness, or injury, or providing respite for your primary caregiver.

Factors to Consider in Hiring Private Caregivers

There are a number of factors to consider in hiring outside help. If you have already established that private caregivers are allowed in your place of residence, the next step is to consider what kind of care you need. It is fairly easy to determine whether you require home care or home health care, but exactly what types of things do you want help with? Before hiring a caregiver, make sure you know what you want. Setting expectations will help the caregiver succeed.

Another major consideration is, of course, cost. Most home care and home health care recipients pay privately or through long-term care insurance. Rates for home care and home health services vary widely, and depend largely upon where you live, the services that you require, and how much assistance you need.

Generally, you will pay a premium for hiring caregivers through an agency rather than hiring privately. This is partly because agencies conduct the initial legwork of prescreening candidates, running background and reference checks, and matching qualified caregivers to your needs. In addition, agencies that employ their caregivers (so that you are the client, not the direct employer) provide ongoing services rather than simply referral and placement. These agencies pay their caregivers and deduct the appropriate taxes, and provide necessary insurance and ongoing supervision and management. If the caregiver they send is not a good fit or must be absent on a day that you need care, the agency will send a replacement. Therefore, while going through an agency can cost more than hiring a caregiver yourself, it can also save you a considerable amount of time and effort both upfront and later.

Finally, there are special insurance considerations for having a caregiver work in your home. First, you may want to consider getting worker's compensation insurance. If your caregiver is injured on the job, you could be liable for related medical expenses, including disability coverage. Worker's Comp protects both you and your employee. If you would like to insure specific personal items in your home, check your homeowner's policy to see if there is any existing protection for theft. If not, ask your insurance agent whether you can extend coverage to include specific items. Your agent will also be able to advise you on what kind of worker's compensation policy you need for a caregiver who works in your home.

If the caregiver will be providing transportation, such as taking you to doctor's appointments, or even just running errands on your behalf, find out whether she has adequate liability insurance coverage. If she gets into a car accident while performing a job-related task, you could be held liable for the damages even if you are not in the car at the time of the accident.

Finally, as an employer of a home caregiver, you could be responsible for purchasing unemployment insurance if your state requires it. That means if you fire your caregiver, she would be entitled to collect unemployment until she finds a new job or until the coverage runs out. Full-service agencies are the only avenue of finding and hiring a caregiver that typically provides insurance coverage for all of these scenarios (with the possible exception of unemployment insurance, where it is not required by law). Read more about full-service agencies later in this chapter.

Finding and Hiring Caregivers

There are several methods for finding and hiring a professional caregiver. You can do it yourself or go through a referral agency or full-service agency. Caregivers can work in your home as an independent contractor, as your employee, or as an employee of the agency they work for.

No matter what route you go for hiring a private caregiver, before you proceed you'll need to identify exactly what kind of help you need. Writing this down in detail is an imperative step in working with private caregivers. Part of this involves job description, but it is just as important to specify your preferences and expectations. If you use an agency to find a caregiver, this list will come in handy for helping them find a suitable match. And if you hire someone on your own, you can refer to this list during the screening and interviewing process, and use it to create a working care plan. Here are some factors to consider in compiling your personal needs list:

- What days or how often do you need a caregiver? Do you expect this to change in the near future?

- What are the hours of the job?

- How long do you expect to need a caregiver (e.g., two weeks, temporarily, indefinitely)?

- What duties does the job entail? How frequently should they be performed?

- Is there any specialized care you require (e.g., incontinence, physical therapy, etc.)?

- Do you have a preference between a male or female caregiver?

- Do you require a caregiver who is bilingual?

- Are there any house rules that you would like to establish (e.g., no visitors, no smoking in the house)?

You can find private-hire caregivers by a variety of means. As independent contractors, how they promote their services is different from person to person. Common methods of connecting with a private-hire caregiver include getting personal or word-of-mouth recommendations, searching job boards such as Craigslist.org or Monster.com, and perusing the classified section of your local newspaper. You can also place your own ad for a caregiver in these forums.

Independent contractors are responsible for reporting their wages and paying their own taxes. If the caregiver works in your home as an employee, however, you have certain obligations as an employer, including withholding payroll taxes from each paycheck. If you employ your caregiver as a household employee, you may find it useful to use payroll software or an on-demand payroll service for this purpose. Two sites that offer payroll software and payroll services are www.eldercarepay.com and www.paycycle.com. The current tax laws have some influence over whether a caregiver is considered an independent contractor or a household employee. In 2009, if you pay a caregiver wages of less than $1,700, then you do not have to report or pay Social Security or Medicare taxes on those wages. In addition to these responsibilities, the IRS holds individuals employers responsible for unemployment compensation and interest on any payments owed, and if you are found to be in violation, you could face possible civil fines of up to $100,000.

For more information on your responsibility as an employer and reporting taxes for a household employee, see Appendix B.

If you choose to hire a private-hire caregiver, either as a household employee or an independent contractor, we strongly suggest that you conduct a background check before hiring that person. You can do this yourself or hire an attorney or private investigator to do it for you. You can also control the extent of the search. At a minimum, ask for at least three references, and find out how many years the candidate has worked as a caregiver. In addition, if the caregiver will be providing transportation, check to be sure that she has a valid driver's license and clean driving record with DMV. For a more thorough check, you may also choose to request a credit report and search county, state, and/or federal criminal records. Before performing a background search on an applicant, however, the law requires that you must obtain written consent from that person.

Many states have an official elder-abuse registry or database. There is no federal regulation that mandates states maintain this type of registry, so the information you find and the agency it is managed by may vary from state to state. To find out if there is an elder-abuse registry in your state, call Adult Protective Services (APS). They are typically managed by APS or another state agency. To be prudent, also check your state's sex offender registry. You can find links to your state registry by visiting www.prevent-abuse-now.com.

Referral agencies are essentially intermediaries. They screen caregivers and run a criminal background check and reference check, and will match you with a qualified caregiver, but they do not provide ongoing supervision. In fact, once you hire a caregiver through a referral agency, your relationship with the agency ends. It is like hiring a de facto private-hire caregiver. Like a private hire, if the person is considered your household employee, you are responsible for paying the caregiver directly and withholding taxes from each paycheck. Also like a private hire, you, not the agency, supervise the caregiver.

Full-service agencies screen and employ their caregivers. The screening process is usually very extensive; it behooves these agencies to have a staff of competent, experienced caregivers to match with their clients. Because your relationship with the agency continues after a caregiver has begun working in your home, ongoing customer satisfaction is a guiding principle.

If you choose to go with a full-service agency to find a caregiver, ask how many years it has been in business. Fewer years aren't necessarily a bad sign, but a lengthier service history can be an indicator of stability and overall customer satisfaction. Ask for references. Check with the Better Business Bureau (www.bbb.org) to see whether any complaints have been filed against the agency. Also make sure the agency is licensed and bonded. Ask if you don't know; this is a crucial piece of information. Licensed agencies can only hire certified or licensed caregivers. And signing a contract with a bonded agency protects you against theft and property damage that may occur. A fidelity bond is a type of insurance that protects you from losses due to dishonest or fraudulent acts caused by an employee. Fidelity bonds are sometimes called theft insurance, but may also be known by other names such as dishonesty bonds or trade guarantee bonds.

Full-service home care and home health agencies typically provide the following services:

- Criminal background checks

- Multiple reference checks

- Worker's compensation insurance

- Liability insurance and/or fidelity bond to cover theft or financial loss

- Pay caregivers directly, including withholding applicable payroll taxes

- Will find a replacement caregiver at your request or when your assigned caregiver is sick

- Ongoing caregiver supervision after hire

Just as the staff would in a long-term care setting, home care and home health agencies conduct an initial needs assessment of new clients and use the information to draft their care plan. To complete a needs assessment, a representative from the agency will visit you in person, interview you, and examine your home if necessary. A basic assessment addresses the following points:

- Your physical health

- List of medications

- Specific duties to be performed

- Home safety

- Quality-of-life issues

Your care plan will explain your needs and identify ways to meet them, which includes setting specific goals and priorities. Care plans are usually reassessed every month and as needed. The care plan is very important even if you only require private caregiving temporarily, as it is a tool for measuring your progress and noting other changes in your health.

If you hire a caregiver through an agency, you will be required to sign a contract. Read it carefully. If any verbal promises were made to you during the consultation process, request that they be incorporated into the contract before you sign.

Finally, the single-most important thing you can do in working with a caregiver in your home (no matter how you found him and no matter who the employer is) is to encourage and practice good communication. Communication is by far the most effective means of establishing mutual understanding, trust, and respect, and of preventing and resolving conflict. If you have set clear expectations and they are not being met, reiterate what it is you expect and ask your caregiver to make the appropriate changes.

Check in with your caregiver regularly to make sure his expectations are being met as well. A person who is content and satisfied in his working environment is apt to do a much better job.

It's a good idea to hold informal meetings regularly, say once a week or once a month, depending on how long you require help and how involved your care plan is. You can invite family members if you wish, or a family member can hold the meeting with your caregiver instead. Ask if there is anything that you can do to help the caregiver do his job that you are not doing now.

Give your caregiver the tools to succeed, including a comfortable, designated place for a break if shifts are long. If you are a direct employer, then you may choose to provide your employee with benefits or job perks, such as modest bonuses, thank-you gifts, or travel reimbursement. Small measures of appreciation go a long way.

If you currently live in a senior housing arrangement, or are about to move into one, chances are you will work with many other staff members in addition to the CNAs, nurses, and administrators described in this chapter. From therapists to feeding assistants, doctors, activity directors, beauticians, dietitians, social workers, and more, lots of facilities employ lots of different staff members. For brevity and practicality, we have included the staff members whom you will likely interact with the most regularly, and who are most likely to directly affect your experience. The real key to working with any caregiver or staff member of senior housing is establishing and maintaining a positive working relationship. If you can do that, you will get the best results.

Chapter 14

Troubleshooting and Resolving Problems

First, a disclaimer: this chapter isn't meant to offer solutions to every problem that you may encounter along the way. To do that would not possible. There are simply too many ever-changing factors and unique situations. This chapter will, however, address common issues that new residents of senior housing face, and offer tried-and-true suggestions for resolving problems that arise.

Even when you plan ahead, research diligently, and are as accommodating as you can possibly be, there are still events that are out of your control. Problems occur. That is a fact of life. What you *can* control is how you deal with the problems you encounter. Emphasizing and maintaining good communication between you, staff members, and your family (as appropriate) is essential in avoiding problems and resolving conflicts that are unavoidable.

Sometimes the process of resolving the problem can be just as frustrating as the initial trouble, particularly if you don't know where to go, what to do, or whom to talk to. This chapter will explore some of the options that are available to you for resolving and reporting problems in your new living situation.

Agencies and Organizations That Can Help

If after reading this chapter you are still unsure of what to do, consider getting help from an objective source, preferably a live person with whom you can speak on the phone or schedule a face-to-face meeting. There are a number of groups that can answer questions or concerns about problems in your new living situation. If they cannot help you directly, they will advise you on next steps to take. These groups include the following:

- The Center for Medicare and Medicaid Services (CMS)

- The National Citizens' Coalition for Nursing Home Reform (NCCNHR)

- Your local Area Agency on Aging

- Your local long-term care ombudsman office

You will find contact information for all of these organizations in Appendix C.

Settling Disputes

No matter what your new living arrangement, there will be a period of adjustment. Hopefully as you settle in, minor irritations and complications will sort themselves out. But if they do not, there are things you can do to resolve them. You have the right to a living environment that is safe and comfortable, and, we hope, reasonably pleasant.

It's common for problems to arise in a shared situation with a roommate. Whether the problem involves the incompatibility of your schedules (you like to rise early; your roommate keeps you up at night), phone issues (she talks too loud or hogs the phone), or privacy issues involving sex and intimacy, you're not the first person to have experienced these problems.

The best tool you have for settling disputes is your own voice. Speak up if you have a problem. The issue may not be apparent to others until you bring it to their attention. You may find that many conflicts can be resolved with a simple conversation. Here are some quick examples and tips for resolving common problems:

- If it's a problem with your roommate, give that person the respect of talking to her first. She may not be aware that her actions are making you uncomfortable.

- If you have a problem with another resident who is bothering you, ask the person to stop. If he does not, report his behavior to a staff member.

- If you have a problem with a staff member, determine whether it is appropriate to speak with the staff member directly to resolve the issue. If it is not, bring your problem to a member of facility management for help.

- If you have a problem with your care, bring the issue up with your caregiver. If the problem is not resolved, talk to the director of nursing or the administrator.

Typically, senior housing arrangements that also offer long-term care services have more channels for reporting problems than independent living. Therefore, if you are in an independent living arrangement, some of the options for reporting problems that are presented in this chapter may not be available to you. However, you still have rights as a private citizen and as a renter.

If the problem is with your apartment, report it to your landlord. If your landlord doesn't respond in a timely manner, remind him of the problem in writing, and keep a copy of your letter so that you have a record. After that, if there is still no response or adequate resolution, call the renter's board in your community to explore other options. If you cannot resolve the problem on your own, call your local Area Agency on Aging. They will be happy to provide advice and referrals to someone who can help you.

What Are My Options?

There are a number of ways to go about resolving problems in your new living situation. Among these are informal methods, such as going directly to the person who is responsible for the issue, and attempting to resolve the problem through conversation, and more formalized procedures such as filing a grievance. In general, it's best to start with the simplest method possible and see if you get results. If you don't, then move on to the next step until your problem is resolved. Use the guidelines in this chapter along with your best judgment; obviously, if your problem is very serious, such as abuse or neglect, you should report it right away to the proper authorities.

Starting at the Source of the Problem

First talk to the person who is the cause of your problem or who is responsible for it. For example, if you have a problem with your care, talk to the caregiver, nurse, or certified nurse's aide. If the problem still is not resolved after directly communicating your concern, escalate your complaint by taking it to that person's supervisor, the facility's social worker, director of nursing, or medical director. You can also talk to your doctor regarding concerns over your care.

Before you do this, however, here is something to keep in mind: no one likes to be told she is doing something wrong, or worse, doing something that hurts or offends another person. In situations where the person may be unaware of the problem, such as an unwitting roommate, try to give the benefit of the doubt, and be considerate of that person's feelings. She may be very embarrassed that her actions have affected you this way, and simply addressing the problem may be enough to make it disappear. Kindly request that the person stop the offending behavior, and if appropriate, suggest an alternative or compromise.

Addressing your complaint to a staff member (or member of management, if the person causing the problem is a staff member) is another option, but if you skip going directly to the source, you may cause further embarrassment and even resentment on the other person's part. Avoid unnecessarily creating a cycle of tension, which doesn't do anyone any good. Do what makes the best sense for the situation. If you bring the complaint to the attention of a staff member, ask that he be discreet in helping you reach a resolution.

Taking It Up with Resident or Family Councils

If informal conversation doesn't get you anywhere, consider trying to resolve your problem through other means, such as bringing it to the attention of the resident council or family council. The old adage about there being strength in numbers certainly applies here. Most facilities are very responsive to resident and family councils.

The primary reason these groups exist is to give members an opportunity to discuss issues and concerns regarding the facility's policies and operations. The facility must listen to and act upon grievances (and recommendations if applicable) reported by the councils.

If you are not comfortable sharing your problem with a group, then the next step is to file a complaint following the facility's grievance procedure.

Filing a Grievance

Nursing homes and assisted living facilities have set procedures for filing a formal complaint, which is known as a grievance. The process will vary by state and by facility, but here are some general things you should know about filing a grievance.

First, you have the right to make a complaint without fear of punishment or retribution. Second, the facility must take action to resolve the problem. And finally, grievances are also investigated by parties independent of the facility, and may include the licensing agency and your local long-term care ombudsman.

You also have the right to file a grievance about any matter that is protected by law. Among other things, this includes abuse and neglect, mistreatment by staff or residents, improper transfer and discharge, unlawful eviction, understaffing, poor or inadequate care, violations of your rights, and safety concerns.

You can make things a whole lot easier on everyone involved, including yourself, by doing several things. Start by documenting the facts of the situation (or "the who, what, when, where, and how"): state what happened, where it took place, the manner in which it occurred, the parties involved, and the date(s) and time(s) of the conflict. Be as specific and as factual as you can and try to keep emotions out of it. Then state your desired outcome: what is it that you do and do not want? Document this, too. As possible, suggest solutions and compromises. Complaining will only get you so far; follow through by making it possible to get to a resolution that works for everyone.

Reporting a Complaint to the Long-Term Care Ombudsman

The Older Americans Act of 1978 is a federal law that mandates states to operate long-term care ombudsman programs for residents of long-term care facilities, which includes assisted living facilities, nursing homes, and those components that exist within CCRCs.

Ombudsmen are resident advocates who respond to complaints and concerns made by or on behalf of long-term care residents. Resident care issues, residents' rights, and quality-of-life issues routinely register among the top complaints registered on behalf of residents in both assisted living and nursing homes.

The primary function of the long-term care ombudsman program as mandated by law is to identify, investigate, and resolve resident complaints. Other functions include "protecting residents' legal rights, advocating for systemic change, providing information and consultation to residents and their families, and publicizing issues of importance to residents."

Ombudsmen do not have the direct authority to require action by a facility. However, they are very effective agents of change and can help you in a variety of ways, including the following:

- Suggesting aging-in-place solutions to help prevent an unnecessary or premature move

- Giving advice on finding and choosing a long-term care facility

- Explaining how nursing home inspections work and what the reports of the results mean

- Answering questions about residents' rights

- Assisting with family and resident councils

- Helping you file a complaint and helping achieve a resolution to your problem

- Connecting you with legal assistance when necessary

There are more than 50 long-term care ombudsman programs operating in all 50 states, the District of Columbia, Guam, and Puerto Rico. A full-time ombudsman administers the program at the state level, with local ombudsmen who work regionally. To find an ombudsman near you, call the Eldercare Locator at 1-800-677-1116 or see Appendix C for more information on long-term care ombudsman programs.

Alternative Dispute Resolution

Alternative dispute resolution generally refers to a variety of methods for settling disputes outside of the courtroom. Some of the most common methods include negotiation, mediation, and arbitration.

Unlike litigation, all methods of alternative dispute resolution must be entered into consensually (unless it is court-mandated). Another difference is the room for flexibility in the alternative dispute-resolution process. For example, it can be used as an independent alternative to an official judicial process, or it can be used as an adjunct.

Exceedingly heavy court caseloads, the rising costs of litigation, and the lengthy commitments that may be required for a court case have all paved the way for a significant increase in the use of alternative dispute resolution in various types of cases. In fact, many courts now require that parties try alternative dispute resolution before allowing the case to be tried in court.

There are a number of reasons that you may find alternative dispute resolution a more attractive option than litigation. First, it gives both parties greater control over the process and outcome of the resolution. Also it tends to be a more cooperative, less contentious, and much less expensive process than litigation. And finally, because it is conducted privately, there is a guarantee of privacy and confidentiality in alternative dispute resolution. The final decision does not become public record.

Litigation

If all other methods of conflict resolution fail, you do have the option of filing a lawsuit. For most problems, litigation is the method of last resort. It is costly, lengthy, contentious, and can be incredibly draining on an emotional level. In addition, there is the risk that you could lose your case in court. If you have ever had the misfortune of being involved in a lawsuit, then you probably know all of this already.

However, litigation may be appropriate for certain types of disputes for which you have not been able to reach a resolution. Some of the advantages of litigation include bringing public attention to the conflict and being awarded damages (i.e., financial compensation).

If you do not have an attorney, you may wish to find one who specializes in the type of problem you have, has a history of handling similar matters, and who is well versed in the body of case law on that topic. The National Academy of Elder Law Attorneys (NAELA) is a good place to start. NAELA is a nonprofit organization whose membership comprises attorneys in the public and private sectors who specialize in elder law concerns that range from health law and mental health law, to neglect, elder abuse and fraud, and more. For more information or to locate an elder law attorney who is a NAELA member, visit www.naela.org or call 520-881-4005.

Legal Considerations

As an individual, a citizen, and as a resident of a long-term care facility, there are various protections are available to you under the law, including basic human rights, civil rights, and residents' rights. You may exercise these rights at any time. If you feel your rights have been violated, call the long-term care ombudsman for advice on what to do.

A basic but critical legal matter that all new residents of senior housing must consider is planning for incapacitation. None of us wants to think about experiencing terminal illness or being diagnosed with Alzheimer's or suffering from a terrible accident that leaves us incapacitated. But it is crucial to consider this possibility, because if it happens, you want to be prepared—if not simply for your own sake, then for the sake of those around you who would be charged with making decisions on your behalf. Planning ahead so that you can make your wishes known will give you peace of mind now—and your loved ones peace of mind later, in the event that they must ensure your wishes are honored.

Essential Legal Documents: Advance Directives

Expect the best, and prepare for the worst: this bit of advice has never been truer than when it comes to preparing legal documents that express your wishes on serious matters regarding your health care. Advance directives therefore might be best described as the best solution in a worst-case scenario.

But here is a better working definition: advance directives are legal documents that provide guidance for medical and health care decisions. You sign an advance directive when you are competent to make such decisions on your own behalf, and they are to be used in the event that you become incompetent to do so. For example, people who are diagnosed with early-stage Alzheimer's are instructed to prepare advance directives so that their wishes are clearly spelled out before they are unable to communicate them verbally or in writing. Advance directives spare your loved ones from having to make serious decisions (made extremely difficult when they are based on best guesses rather than documented wishes) about your health care during a time of crisis. It also prevents anxiety and potential conflict on the part of loved ones over what you would have wanted.

There are variations between states in the language and provisions of some advance directives, so make sure the ones you choose are legally binding in the state where you reside (and verify that your documents are valid if you move to senior housing in a different state).

A living will is one of the most common types of advance directives. It is sometimes called a directive to physicians. A living will specifies your health care preferences, and usually specifies in particular your preference to either be kept alive by artificial means (such as a respirator) or be allowed to die if you become disabled beyond a reasonable expectation of recovery. Both your doctor and a second doctor must certify that your condition is terminal and that you are unable to make your own decisions before the living will can be effected.

Another common advance directive is a durable power of attorney for health care. A durable power of attorney for health care specifies the person you wish to make health decisions on your behalf if you should become incapacitated. Similarly to a living will, a durable power of attorney for health care cannot be used unless your attending physician and another doctor certify that you are unable to make decisions on your own. Some states allow an accredited psychologist to make the second certification.

It's a smart move to have both a living will and a durable power of attorney so that all of your bases are covered.

A do not resuscitate (DNR) order is a third type of advance directive, which specifies your request that you do not want to have cardiopulmonary resuscitation (CPR) performed on you if your heart stops or if you stop breathing. Without a DNR, medical workers will use CPR to help all patients whose heart has stopped or who have stopped breathing. If you do not want CPR performed on you under these conditions, you can fill out a DNR document, or tell your doctor to record your wish on your medical chart. DNRs are accepted by doctors, hospitals, and long-term care facilities in all 50 states.

Because they are considered long-term care providers, assisted living facilities, nursing homes, and CCRCs must disclose their policies regarding the implementation of advance directives that limit the delivery of medical services or care before you sign any contract. If you do not know these policies, find out what they are.

A final note on advance directives: the hardest part is thinking about the possibility that you might one day be unable to communicate your own choices. Obtaining and filling out the documents is ridiculously easy. Do it.

Role of Family Members

There are a number of ways that family members can help you resolve problems that you encounter in your new living arrangement. If you live in an assisted living facility, nursing home, or CCRC, then family members, legal guardians, and even friends may participate in family councils. Facilities with family councils are typically very responsive to suggestions or concerns made by the group.

In addition, at your request or as appropriate, family members should acquaint themselves with the facility's policies. As they visit you and become acquainted with facility staff, it should be a natural progression for them to talk to staff on your behalf if you are not comfortable doing so yourself. Many minor complaints can be resolved with a frank conversation. Family members may also report a complaint on your behalf to the local long-term care ombudsman.

No matter where you reside and what role you would like them to take, family members can help you by taking an active role or a supporting role in helping you resolve problems.

If You Are Reading This Book on Behalf of a Loved One

Thank you. Also here are some words of advice:

- Try to gauge the weight of the complaint. If it is serious, follow up with a plan of action. Determine what your loved one wants from you. Does he simply want to vent frustrations, or is action required? If it is the former, practice good listening skills, be supportive and comfort the person as needed. Even if the complaint is minor, your reaction is important. This period of adjustment is largely psychological. The importance of keeping up morale cannot be stressed enough. If it is the latter, get moving.

- If your loved one presents a legitimate complaint, address your concern to the staff member it involves (if applicable) or a member of management or the facility administrator. Keep it as factual as possible; getting emotional over a legitimate complaint is easy to do and it is a natural reaction, but it helps no one, and may even hurt your chances of getting the complaint resolved to your satisfaction. If the complaint is serious and not resolved by presenting the facts to a senior employee of the facility, file a formal complaint. The facility is required to make the process of filing a complaint (a.k.a. a grievance) public and available to applicants, residents, and family members of both.

- Keep your loved one in the loop as a complaint is being resolved. Give her status updates. Having that information and being able to see that progress is being made will give the resident a feeling of control rather than helplessness. This is very important.

- Be in touch regularly so that you monitor how your loved one is adjusting, and spot problems before they become serious. Visit when you can, call regularly, and send letters or cards in between. If your loved one is comfortable with technology (and has sufficient room in his residence), buy a basic computer printer or fax machine to keep in touch via e-mail or fax.

- Deal with problems as they arise; don't wait for a more convenient time. There probably won't be one. Also, your responsiveness will mean the world to your loved one, who is likely to be reassured that you are "there" for her.

- Pay attention to nonverbal cues such as loss of appetite, lack of interest in activities that are usually enjoyed, and other noncharacteristic behavioral changes, which could signal a problem even if your loved one doesn't complain. Isolation and depression are common among new residents who are having trouble adapting to and accepting their new environment. Make sure he doesn't simply withdraw during this period of transition. Engage staff members to help you with this when you can't be there.

- Don't be quick to dismiss complaints if they seem insignificant to you. Even minor complaints can be hugely significant in a new resident's mind, especially if she thinks it is the new status quo that she must get used to. Be patient and empathetic. Sometimes having someone you love take the time to listen to you is enough, and no other action is required.

Financial Implications

With the exceptions of alternative dispute resolution and litigation, the various methods of conflict resolution outlined in this chapter are all free. The cost of alternative dispute resolution and litigation both vary enormously, and are dependent upon many factors, including attorney's fees and time spent working on your case. Make sure you discuss all fees up front before moving forward, and get documentation of the fees you have discussed.

If you decide to move out of your senior housing arrangement, in most cases you will be responsible for relocating costs and you may also be responsible for fees associated with breaking your lease or agreement.

What to Do in a Case of Abuse or Neglect

There are all types of problems you may encounter in your new living arrangement. When the situation is very serious and poses immediate threat or harm, informal methods of conflict resolution may not be enough.

If you have been abused or neglected, report it immediately to the proper authorities. This may include contacting your local long-term care ombudsman, local law enforcement, facility authorities, your family, the Centers for Medicare & Medicaid Services (CMS), and Adult Protective Services (APS).

Adult Protective Services provides protective and supportive services for elderly, disabled, and incapacitated adults who are victims of abuse, exploitation, or neglect. There are APS programs that operate in all 50 states. To find your state APS program, visit www.apsnetwork.org or call the Eldercare Locator at 1-800-677-1116. If it is an emergency, call 911.

If, after trying all possible methods of resolving your conflict, the facility you've chosen still isn't a good fit for you, then it may be time to resume your search for another senior housing arrangement that is a better fit. If you were referred to the living arrangement, it's important to tell the referrer the reasons why the place you chose did not work out for you. Think of it as good karma for the next person who comes along asking for a senior housing referral.

Appendix A

Glossary

Active Adult Retirement Community *See* independent living.

activities of daily living (ADLs) Personal hygiene, grooming, bathing, dressing, toileting, feeding, transferring, and medication management.

administrator A licensed professional who manages the daily operations of an assisted living facility or nursing home.

advance directive A legal document stating your health care preferences, to be used if and when you become unable to make your own decisions due to incapacitation. There are different types of advance directives. Some senior housing providers require applicants have certain advance directives in place prior to moving in.

aging in place The concept of remaining in one's place of residence despite changing health or cognitive needs. Concept includes measures that support aging in place.

alternative dispute resolution Any of a number of methods for resolving disputes outside of the government judicial process; may include negotiation, mediation, collaborative law, and arbitration. May be used to settle disputes between residents, and between residents and senior housing providers and/or staff members as an alternative to litigation.

assessment An evaluation of one's health and/or cognitive status. May also include an estimation of emotional and social capabilities. Usually performed by a doctor, geriatric care manager, or interdisciplinary team of medical and health professionals.

assisted living facility Residential housing that offers supportive services, custodial care, and usually meals and housekeeping, in a homelike environment. For people who do not require 24-hour care. May also be known as residential care for the elderly.

assistive technology   Any tool or product that helps a person to perform an activity that was impossible or difficult to do without assistance.

care plan   In a nursing home, a detailed plan that explains a resident's health and cognitive needs and proposed methods of meeting them. Based on an assessment and updated periodically or as necessary.

citation   Formal statement issued to a nursing home when it is fined for a deficiency. Also known as a deficiency citation.

CNA   Certified nurse's aide. Also known as certified nursing assistants.

community spouse (Medicaid)   Refers to the spouse who is at home while the other spouse is in a long-term care facility.

congregate housing   A category of independent living that usually offers optional services including meal plans, laundry, transportation, and housekeeping services. May also be known as congregate living.

conservator   An individual or institution that has been designated to take over and protect the interests of an incompetent person.

continuing care contract   *See* Type B Contract/Modified Contract.

continuing care retirement community (CCRC)   A residential community that offers a continuum of care, usually including independent living, assisted living, and nursing home care in a single location. *See also* life care community.

convalescent home   *See* nursing home.

culture change (in nursing homes)   A movement toward changing traditional nursing home culture from "institutional" to more homelike living, with the primary goal of improving residents' quality of life. This may include allowing residents greater choice and flexibility over their personal schedules, eating, and activities. It may also involve changing the physical environment to support these initiatives. Also referred to as resident-centered care or resident-directed care.

custodial care   Nonmedical care that provides assistance with the activities of daily living.

deductible medical expenses   Qualified medical and dental expenses for which you may claim a tax deduction.

deficiency   Failure to meet state and federal minimum standards for care or fire safety regulation, formally recorded by the nursing home inspection team when a nursing home is found to be noncompliant or in violation.

deficiency citation   *See* citation.

director of nursing (DON)   Person at the head of nursing staff who sets nursing policies, and is responsible for nursing home compliance with state and federal regulations. Usually works with medical director.

do not resucitate (DNR) order   A type of advance directive that requests that resuscitation should not be attempted in the event of cardiac or respiratory arrest. You can fill out an advance directive DNR form, or initiate a DNR by requesting your doctor add it to your medical record. If you do not have a DNR, hospital and emergency workers are required by law to attempt resuscitation if your heart has stopped and/or if you have stopped breathing.

durable power of attorney   A legal document that designates a party to act on your behalf in the event that you become incapacitated. Also known as a letter of attorney.

durable power of attorney for health care decisions   A legal document that designates a party to make health care decisions on your behalf in the event that you become incapacitated.

elimination period (for LTCI)   A specified number of days before your policy benefits will begin to pay, during which you are responsible for expenses. Also known as the waiting period. *See also* long-term care insurance (LTCI).

end-of-life care   *See* hospice.

estate planning   The process of disposing of one's estate (i.e., all assets owned at the time of death). May include a will, power of attorney, living will, and, in some cases, a trust.

facility culture   The common attitudes, values, and goals shared by residents and staff; also, the traditions and practices that characterize the senior housing community.

family council   An organized group of relatives and friends of assisted living or nursing home residents who meet regularly to discuss mutual concerns and issues pertaining to the facility and its residents.

fidelity bond   A type of insurance that protects businesses and employers from losses due to fraudulent or dishonest acts by an employee. Also known as theft insurance, dishonesty bonds, or trade guarantee bonds. Full-service home care and home health care agencies typically have this kind of coverage to protect against damage or loss that may occur in your home.

fiduciary   A person who has a responsibility to act in good faith and trust on the part of a client.

first-day deductible (Medicare)   The amount that you must pay for the first day of hospitalization under Medicare Part A before your benefits become effective. *See also* Medicare; Medicare Part A Hospital Insurance.

geriatric care manager   A professional advocate who works with older adults and their families to resolve problems and suggest solutions with regard to any number of aging issues, but with a particular focus on senior housing and long-term care.

grievance   A formal complaint filed against a facility.

guardian   A person who is designated with the protective care over another person or that person's property.

home care   Custodial care provided in one's home or in a long-term care facility as additional care is needed.

home health care   Skilled nursing care provided in one's home (requires a doctor's prescription).

hospice   An in-patient medical facility or program for the terminally ill that focuses on providing comfort care and meeting the physical and emotional needs of the dying. Also known as end-of-life care.

independent living   Residential housing for seniors who do not require personal or medical care. Usually offers standard safety features in the residence, and may offer recreational activities, meal plans, and housekeeping services. May also be known as senior apartments, retirement communities, or congregate living. Referred to as elderly housing for government-subsidized programs.

information sharing (CCRCs)   The process by which CCRCs share information with residents, including information on community operations and finances. May include updates via a resident council, formal reports, quarterly updates, or meetings, or a combination of these methods.

intake meeting   A meeting between facility staff and the applicant, prior to moving in, to determine the applicant's needs, desires, abilities, and preferences in order to draft a care plan (in nursing homes) or service plan (in assisted living).

letter of attorney   *See* durable power of attorney.

life care community   A type of CCRC that offers the Type A Extended Care contract exclusively. *See also* continuing care retirement community (CCRC).

life care contract   *See* Type A Contract/Extended Contract.

living will   A legal document that specifies the medical treatment and/or procedures you would or would not want performed on you in the event that you become unable to communicate your wishes. Life support is usually the primary focus, but a living will may also detail spiritual and emotional preferences. A living will is one type of advance directive, and in some states may be called a directive to physicians. *See also* advance directive.

long-term care facility   Any facility that provides long-term care (e.g., custodial or skilled nursing care), such as an assisted living facility or nursing home.

long-term care insurance (LTCI)   Private insurance that helps pay long-term care expenses, including custodial care at home, adult day care, adult day health care, care in an assisted living facility, and care in a nursing home, depending on the policy.

long-term care ombudsman   An advocate for residents of long-term care facilities. Ombudsmen help resolve problems between residents and facilities by acting as a trusted intermediary; common issues include quality of care, food, finances, medical care, and residents' rights.

look-back period (Medicaid)   The period in which Medicaid officials may review your financial transactions (from the preceding five years) to ensure that you meet Medicaid's eligibility requirements.

LPN   Licensed practical nurse. In some states, may be called a LVN.

LVN   Licensed vocational nurse. In some states, may be called a LPN.

Medicaid   A state-operated public health program for eligible low-income people and families with limited resources. Programs and coverage vary from state to state.

medical director   A person who oversees all aspects of resident medical care at a nursing home and is responsible for setting and implementing policies related to medical care at the facility. Also coordinates with residents' individual primary care physicians, and/or acts as residents' primary care physician.

Medicare   A federal health insurance program for people 65 and older, certain disabled people under 65, and people of any age with end-stage renal disease.

Medicare Part A Hospital Insurance   Medicare plan that covers some in-patient hospital care, skilled nursing care, home health care, and hospice care. Benefits are free and automatic once you turn 65.

Medicare Part B Medical Insurance   An optional plan that requires a monthly premium and covers certain medical services, treatments, and necessary medical equipment.

Medicare Part C Medicare Advantage Plan   A Medicare health plan offered by private companies that offer the combined benefits of the Part A and Part B plans, either through a coordinated care plan or medical savings account, to be used in conjunction with a private fee-for-service plan.

Medicare Part D Prescription Drug Plan   An insurance plan offered through insurance companies and other private companies that contract with Medicare and offers prescription drug coverage.

Medicare Supplemental Insurance   *See* Medigap.

medication administration   The process by which a trained medical professional administers prescribed medications to a patient or resident (considered skilled care).

medication management   Procedures for ensuring resident/patient compliance with prescribed drug regimen. May include verbal medication reminders and coordination with resident's doctor (considered custodial care).

Medigap   A type of health insurance policy sold by private insurance companies used to pay costs not covered by Medicare, such as coinsurance, deductibles, and copayments. Ten different policies are available. Also known as Medicare Supplemental Insurance.

nursing home   A medical facility for people who require 24-hour care, which usually offers rehabilitative services, meal plans, laundry, housekeeping services, and planned activities. Also known as a skilled nursing facility.

occupational therapy   A type of therapy that focuses on restoring an individual's ability to independently perform the activities of daily living.

ombudsman   *See* long-term care ombudsman.

PACE (Program of All-Inclusive Care for the Elderly)   A Medicare program that provides continuous care and services for seniors and disabled people 55 or older, with the goal of delaying nursing home placement and enabling program participants to remain at home or continue living in the community for as long as possible.

penalty period   The amount of time that Medicaid withholds payment for nursing home care or other long-term care as penalty for a transfer of assets found to be below market value.

physical therapy   A type of therapy that focuses on restoring an individual's function and strength after an injury or illness.

preventative care   Measures taken to prevent illness or injury, e.g., annual flu shots (as opposed to curative treatments).

private pay   Long-term care expenses that are not covered by insurance and must be paid out of pocket with personal funds. Also known as private payment.

private payment   *See* private pay.

private-duty nurse   A registered nurse who operates as an independent contractor or works for a nursing organization or home health agency, and provides nursing services in a private residential setting, often in a home or at an assisted living residence.

public housing   A program administered by HUD that helps low-income families, seniors, and disabled people find affordable housing; also the actual housing for program participants.

rebate   *See* refund.

refund   The portion of a CCRC entrance fee that is refundable. Refunds are structured in one of three ways: declining scale, partial refund, and full refund. Known in some states as a rebate.

rehabilitation   The process by which one's abilities are restored after a disabling injury or illness.

resident council   An organized group of assisted living or nursing home residents who meet regularly to discuss mutual concerns and issues pertaining to the facility and its policies.

resident-centered care   *See* culture change.

resident-directed care   *See* culture change.

residential care for the elderly   *See* assisted living facility.

respite care   Short-term care that allows a primary caregiver time off from his or her caregiving responsibilities temporarily; may be provided via in-home care, short-term nursing home or assisted living stays, or adult day care.

retirement communities   *See* independent living.

reverse mortgage   A type of mortgage for people 62 and older that enables them to convert home equity into available funds through a line of credit, cash advance, or periodic disbursements. Typically must be repaid with interest when the borrower dies, moves, or sells the home.

RN   Registered nurse.

Section 8 Housing Choice Voucher Program   A HUD-administered program that provides tenant-based rental assistance to low-income families, seniors, and disabled individuals and enables participants to choose their own housing in the private market.

Section 202 Supportive Housing for the Elderly   A federally funded low-income housing program designed specifically for seniors. Many Section 202 housing projects provide basic services such as meal delivery, light housekeeping, and transportation to local health providers.

senior apartment   *See* independent living.

service plan   In assisted living, a detailed plan that explains a resident's health and cognitive needs and proposed methods of meeting them. Based on an assessment and updated periodically or as necessary.

skilled care   *See* skilled nursing care.

skilled nursing care   A combination of medical care and/or rehabilitative services provided on a 24-hour basis, in a skilled nursing facility. Sometimes called skilled care.

skilled nursing facility   *See* nursing home.

snapshot date (Medicaid)   The date that you or your spouse is admitted to a hospital, nursing home, or assisted living facility for an extended stay. Medicaid uses this date to calculate the amount of spending down that is required in order for you to be eligible.

speech therapy   A type of therapy that focuses on restoring a person's ability to communicate using language after suffering a disorder or impairment due to illness.

spending down (Medicaid)   The process of reducing your assets in order to qualify for Medicaid.

state health insurance assistance program (SHIP)   A free program that offers counseling services on health insurance-related topics, with a focus issues affecting seniors.

Supplemental Security Income (SSI)   A program funded by the U.S. Treasury general funds and administered by the Social Security Administration that pays monthly benefits to qualified seniors 65 or older who are blind or disabled.

Type A Contract/Extended Contract (CCRCs)   One of three basic contract types offered by CCRCs, typically the most expensive option; it offers housing, services, and amenities, and unlimited health care for life. Type A contracts are associated with the least amount of risk. Also known as a life care contract.

Type B Contract/Modified Contract (CCRCs)   A CCRC contract that provides specified housing, services, and amenities but limits one's access to long-term health care and nursing services. Type B contracts are associated with a moderate amount of risk. Also known as a continuing care contract.

Type C Contract/Fee-for-Service Contract (CCRCs)   A type of CCRC contract that stipulates payment only for care services that are utilized, and also specifies details of access to health care, housing, services, and amenities. Type C contracts have the highest amount of risk.

Veterans Benefits   A benefits package for veterans and eligible family members that covers primary and preventative care, including hospital and outpatient medical care. Veterans with a service-related disability and veterans who fall below the low-income threshold have top priority. The program is administered by the U.S. Department of Veterans Affairs (VA).

waiting period   *See* elimination period.

will   A legal document that states a person's wishes regarding the disposal of his or her property after death.

Appendix B

Resources

Downloadable Resources

Medicare publishes a number of very helpful publications, which are updated every year or as policies or coverage changes. These can be downloaded for free from the Medicare site at www.Medicare.gov (click on "Find a Medicare Publication"). Here are some of the most popular publications:

- *Choosing a Medigap Policy: A Guide to Health Insurance for People with Medicare*   Extensive guide explains how Medigap policies work, details coverage for the different plans, describes how insurance companies set prices for Medigap policies, and offers information and examples to help you choose the right policy for your needs.

- *If You Need Help Paying Medicare Costs, There Are Programs That Can Help You*   Brochure provides information on Medicare Savings Programs.

- *Medicare and Home Health Care*   Booklet describes Medicare coverage of home health care services.

- *Medicare & You*   Extensive handbook provides an overview of Medicare coverage and benefits, Medicare health plan choices, and your legal rights and protections. Answers frequently asked questions about the Medicare program.

- *Medicare Coverage of Skilled Nursing Facility Care*   Booklet details conditions and extent of Medicare nursing home coverage.

- *Medicare Hospice Benefits*   Booklet details hospice benefits covered by Medicare.

- *Planning for Your Discharge*   Checklist details important information for patients and caregivers who are preparing to leave a hospital, nursing home, or other health care setting.

- *Use Information About Quality on Medicare.gov*   Brochure describes how the Medicare website can help you compare health plans, Medigap policies, prescription drug plans, and assorted health care.

- *Your Guide to Medicare Prescription Drug Coverage*   Booklet describes Medicare coverage for prescription drugs and explains how you can get extra help paying for prescription drug coverage if you have limited income and resources as well as how the Medicare coverage may affect your current prescription drug coverage.

The Social Security Administration publishes a number of guides and brochures in several languages that can be downloaded for free from www.ssa.gov. Click on "Forms and Publications."

Social Security Retirement Benefits   Brochure that outlines everything you need to know about retirement and family benefits. To get a copy of the booklet, call 1-800-772-1213 and ask for Publication No. 05-10035. Or view the booklet online at www.ssa.gov.

The IRS provides several useful publications that can downloaded for free at www.irs.gov/formspubs or ordered by calling 1-800-829-3676, or by writing to this address:

Internal Revenue Service
1201 N. Mitsubishi Motorway
Bloomington, IL 61705-6613

- *IRS Publication 502: Medical and Dental Expenses*   Details deductible medical and dental expenses, and rules and restrictions regarding deducting these expenses.

- *IRS Publication 524: Credit for the Elderly or the Disabled*   Explains the tax credit available to eligible seniors and disabled individuals, including income limits and other eligibility requirements.

- *IRS Publication 915: Introductory Material*   Explains the federal income tax rules for social security benefits and equivalent tier 1 railroad retirement benefits.

- *IRS Publication 926: Hiring Household Employees* Household Employer's Tax Guide (if you hire a private-hire home care worker).

Books

All of the following books are available at www.amazon.com.

Bove, Alexander A., Jr. *The Medicaid Planning Handbook: A Guide to Protecting Your Family's Assets from Catastrophic Nursing Home Costs.* Little, Brown and Company, 1996.

Heiser, K. Gabriel. *How to Protect Your Family's Assets from Devastating Nursing Home Costs: Medicaid Secrets, Third Edition.* Boulder ElderLaw, 2009.

Loverde, Joy. *The Complete Eldercare Planner: Where to Start, Which Questions to Ask, and How to Find Help, Revised & Updated Edition.* Three Rivers Press, 2009.

Rhodes, Linda Colvin, Ed.D. *The Complete Idiot's Guide to Caring for Aging Parents.* Alpha Books, 2001.

Susik, D. Helen. *Hiring Home Caregivers: The Family Guide to In-Home Eldercare.* Impact Publications, 1995.

Internet Resources

ABLEDATA   www.abledata.com
ABLEDATA is a consumer-focused website that reports on and reviews assistive technology and rehabilitation products. The site also features product listings, a Consumer Forum with consumer product reviews, and links to numerous assistive technology resources and companies.

Access America for Seniors   www.seniors.gov
Seniors.gov is a portal where you can browse or search a range of topics of interest to seniors, from housing for seniors to caregivers' resources, consumer protection for seniors, and more. The site also provides direct links to related interests, such as Social Security, the Eldercare Locator, and Medicare.

Administration on Aging (AoA)   www.aoa.gov
Part of the Department of Health and Human Services, the AoA is a federal agency that provides a wide array of home- and community-based services to seniors and family caregivers.
Some of the services and programs provided through the AoA include meal delivery, transportation, legal assistance, and wellness programs; the Long-Term Care Ombudsman Program; the National Center on Elder Abuse; and the Pension Counseling and Information Program. Visit the website for additional information.

Benefits CheckUp   www.benefitscheckup.org
A free, confidential service that helps seniors who have limited income and resources to find benefit programs that help with routine expenses including prescription drug costs, medical bills, meal programs, rent, legal services, heating/energy bills, in-home services, and more.

Consumer Consortium on Assisted Living (CCAL)   www.ccal.org
CCAL is a national consumer advocacy organization that educates residents and families about their rights; supports them in protecting their rights; and works to ensure the quality, affordability, and availability of assisted living to all consumers.

Consumer Reports   www.consumerreports.org
Consumer Reports investigates and reports on issues of interest to consumers of nursing homes and assisted living, and also provides advice on how to find quality residences and recognize common problems with housing and care providers. Search for "nursing homes" and "assisted living."

Department of Housing and Urban Development (HUD)   www.hud.gov
HUD's website offers general consumer information on buying, financing, and selling your home. To learn more about senior-specific housing issues such as reverse mortgages, housing discrimination, and age-restricted housing, visit www.hud.gov/groups/seniors.cfm.

Eldercare Locator   www.eldercare.gov
A service provided by the U.S. Administration on Aging, the Eldercare Locator allows you to search for home and community-based senior support services where you live. The database includes resources for legal assistance, elder abuse prevention services, health insurance counseling, prescription assistance, and more.

ElderCarePay   www.eldercarepay.com
Access downloadable payroll accounting software and IRS-approved wage reporting forms. For employers of household employees such as home care workers.

Financial Planning Association (FPA)   www.fpanet.org
A national advocacy organization, FPA maintains a national database of certified financial planners. Search for a financial professional by location or last name. You can refine your search by choosing from 45 different specialties and 5 options for how planners charge. FPA also offers consumer-focused information about the financial planning process and how to choose a financial planning professional.

GovBenefits   www.GovBenefits.gov
A partnership of federal agencies with information on more than 1,000 benefit and government assistance programs.

IRS   www.irs.gov
Download forms, e-file your taxes, and track your refund online.

Legal Hotlines   www.legalhotlines.org
Maintains a database of senior legal hotlines (defined as hotlines or programs that provide legal advice by phone) for all 50 states.

Medicaid   www.cms.hhs.gov/home/medicaid.asp
The Centers for Medicare & Medicaid Services (CMS) provides information about the Medicaid program, including eligibility, enrollment, benefits and coverage, programs and initiatives, and more.

Medicare   www.medicare.gov
Get information on current Medicare premiums and coinsurance rates, prescription drug coverage, Medicare health plans, and answers to frequently asked questions about the Medicare system. Also find and compare home health agencies, nursing homes (see Nursing Home Compare, below) and hospitals in your area.

National Association of Personal Financial Advisors (NAPFA)
www.napfa.org
NAPFA is a member organization of financial planning professionals. To find a fee-only advisor, or for more information about the financial planning process, visit the "Consumer Information" and "Learning Center" sections.

National Association of State Veterans Homes (NASVH)
www.nasvh.org
A member organization of state veterans homes, NASVH provides information on recent legislation, links to VA programs, and a directory of homes by
state.

National Council on the Aging (NCOA)   www.ncoa.org
An advocacy group dedicated to improving the lives of the nation's older
adults, NCOA focuses its work in five key areas: healthy aging, workforce
development, civic engagement, access to benefits, and long-term services
and support. Among NCOA's numerous programs are Benefits CheckUp (see
Benefits CheckUp, above); My Medicare Matters, an educational program
offering information and support in enrolling in the Medicare Prescription Drug Coverage plan; Respectability, a program that promotes senior
volunteerism through nonprofit organizations; and Wisdom Works, a civic
engagement program.

National Long-Term Care Ombudsman Resource Center
www.ltcombudsman.org
The National Long-Term Care Ombudsman Resource Center provides
support, assistance, and training to the state long-term care ombudsman programs, and provides consumer referrals to local ombudsman programs. Visit
the site to learn more about what ombudsmen can and cannot help you with,
and to learn how you can become a volunteer ombudsman.

Nursing Home Compare   www.medicare.gov/NHCompare/home.asp
A feature of the official Medicare site, Nursing Home Compare enables you
to find and compare nursing homes in your area and across the country. You
can customize and refine your search through a variety of criteria, including
location, overall rating, number of certified beds, ownership type (e.g., for
profit individual or corporation, nonprofit corporation, government-owned,
etc.), and more. Nursing Home Compare also publishes the results of the
nursing homes' latest inspection reports.

Paycycle   www.paycycle.com
Paycycle provides on-demand payroll services for small businesses and
employers of household employees such as professional caregivers.

Senior Law   www.seniorlaw.com
The Senior Law website offers information on a variety of topics of interest to seniors, including elder law, Medicare, Medicaid, guardianship, estate planning, and trusts. The site is sponsored by the law firm of Goldfarb Abrandt Salzman & Kutzin LLP, which specializes in elder law, trusts and estate law, and the rights of the elderly and disabled.

Sex Offender Registries   www.prevent-abuse-now.com/register.htm
Website provides links to state offender registries, information about laws on sex offender registrations, and more.

Social Security Benefits Estimator   www.ssa.gov/estimator
You can use the Retirement Estimator to estimate your retirement benefits if you have enough Social Security credits to qualify for benefits; are not currently receiving Social Security benefits; are not a Medicare beneficiary; are not 62 or older and receiving benefits on someone else's Social Security record (e.g., as a widow); and are not eligible for a pension based on work not covered by Social Security.

Society of Financial Services Professionals   www.financialpro.org
A national network of credentialed financial professionals, the society lists and explains the diverse range of financial credentials and what those designations mean, and provides a wealth of other consumer-focused financial planning information on its website. Visit the site or call the national Consumer Referral Service at 1-888-243-2258 to find a credentialed financial professional in your area.

Vet Homes Foundation   www.vethomesfoundation.org
A national nongovernment and nonprofit foundation whose goal is to assist elderly and infirm veterans through a variety of philanthropic efforts. Learn about programs and how to apply for benefits on the foundation's consumer-friendly site.

Helpful Agencies and Organizations

Administration on Aging (AoA)
Washington, DC 20201
202-619-0724
1-800-677-1116 (Eldercare Locator)
www.aoa.gov

AoA is a federal advocate organization for seniors and their caregivers. To find your local area agency on aging (AAA), call the Eldercare Locator or visit the website.

Alliance for Retired Americans
202-974-8222
1-800-333-7212 (Membership Line)
www.retiredamericans.org

Alliance for Retired Americans organizes advocate groups to lobby legislators on issues affecting seniors, such as problems with Social Security, Medicare, long-term care insurance reform plans, and affordable housing benefits.

Alzheimer's Association
225 N. Michigan Avenue, Floor 17
Chicago, IL 60601-7633
1-800-272-3900 (24/7 Helpline)
www.alz.org

The Alzheimer's Association is a voluntary health organization that focuses on Alzheimer's care, support, research, and awareness. The association offers a variety of resources and programs through its local chapters. Visit the website to locate your local chapter or call the helpline for information, referrals and support.

A.M. Best Company
Ambest Road
Oldwick, NJ 08858
908-439-2200
www.ambest.com

A.M. Best Company is one of the primary rating agencies for the financial and health care industries. The company rates insurers' financial strength and examines their ability to meet its "ongoing insurance policy and contract obligations."

American Association of Homes and Services for the Aging (AAHSA)
2519 Connecticut Avenue, NW
Washington, DC 20008-1520
202-783-2242
www.aahsa.org

AAHSA helps meet the needs of seniors and their families with services offered through its network of 5,700 aging services nonprofit organizations. AAHSA members provide aging services ranging from community and supportive services to housing and health care.

American Association of Retired Persons (AARP)
1-888-687-2277
www.aarp.org

You can find your local AARP chapter by calling or searching online. AARP member benefits and services include discounted credit, health care, insurance, travel, and more.

American Health Quality Association (AHQA)
1155 21st Street NW
Washington, DC 20036
202-331-5790
www.ahqa.org

AHQA is a member organization that represents Quality Improvement Organizations (QIOs) and individual professionals whose work goal is to improve the quality of health care across the country. The QIOs work with nursing homes, hospitals, home health care agencies, and assorted other health care providers to share best practices and identify areas for improvement while providing support. Visit the website to locate the QIO in your state.

Armed Forces Veterans Home Foundation
5211 Auth Road
Suitland, MD 20746
1-800-638-0594
www.vethomesfoundation.org

The Armed Forces Veterans Home Foundation is a national nongovernmental organization that solicits, manages, and disburses grants and other financial awards to agencies nationwide that serve elderly and disabled veterans. The foundation's consumer-friendly website provides information on available programs and benefits.

Assistance League (AL)
818-846-3777
www.assistanceleague.org

Assistance League is a national nonprofit organization with chapters across the U.S. whose member volunteers help seniors in a variety of ways, ranging from companionship and in-person visits to private homes, nursing homes, and hospitals, to coordinating income opportunities for seniors who create handcrafted items.

Assisted Living Federation of America (ALFA)
1650 King Street, Suite 602
Alexandria, VA 22314-2747
703-894-1805
www.alfa.org

ALFA makes referrals to assisted living facilities, and provides free consumer information to help you learn more about assisted living, from costs to regulations, statistics, and more.

Beacon Hill Village
74 Joy Street
Boston, MA 02114
617-723-9713
www.beaconhillvillage.org

A nonprofit member organization, Beacon Hill Village is a NORC in Boston that offers educational workshops and assistance in helping other groups of seniors and interested parties form their own NORCs. Visit the website for details and for a list of established NORCs across the United States.

Better Business Bureau (BBB)
The Council of Better Business Bureaus
4200 Wilson Boulevard, Suite 800
Arlington, VA 22203-1838
703-276-0100
www.bbb.org

The BBB enables consumers to check out a business or file a complaint, and offers assistance with dispute resolution.

CARF-CCAC (Commission on Accreditation of Rehabilitation Facilities/Continuing Care Accreditation Commission)
1730 Rhode Island Avenue, NW
Suite 209
Washington, DC 20036
1-866-888-1122
www.carf.org/aging

CARF-CCAC is a nonprofit accrediting agency for continuing care retirement communities and aging services networks. The agency reviews and grants accreditation to CCRCs across the United States and Canada. Find accredited communities and services by calling or visiting the CARF website.

Center for Medicare Advocacy
P.O. Box 350
Willimantic, CT 06226
860-456-7790
www.medicareadvocacy.org

The Center for Medicare Advocacy is a national nonprofit organization that provides information, education, advocacy, and legal assistance to seniors and disabled individuals to help them access Medicare coverage and health care. The center's website is extremely well organized, consumer-friendly, and covers a breadth of Medicare-related topics.

Centers for Medicare & Medicaid Services (CMS)
7500 Security Boulevard
Baltimore, MD 21244-1850
1-800-MEDICARE
1-877-486-2048 (TTY)
www.cms.gov
www.medicare.gov

CMS is a clearinghouse for information about the Medicare and Medicaid programs, with comprehensive sections on legislation, regulations and guidance, research and statistics, outreach and education, resources and tools, and more.

Consumer Consortium on Assisted Living (CCAL)
2342 Oak Street
Falls Church, VA 22046
703-533-8121
www.ccal.org

CCAL is a consumer advocacy group that offers free consumer information and links to state licensing agencies.

Department of Housing and Urban Development (HUD)
451 7th Street S.W.
Washington, DC 20410
202-708-1112
202-708-1455 (TTY)
www.hud.gov

The HUD website offers information on buying, financing, and selling your home, as well as information that is specific to seniors. Call or go online to connect with a HUD-approved counseling agency that can answer questions and give you advice on defaults, foreclosures, credit issues, reverse mortgages, and more. Find a HUD office near you by visiting the website.

Department of Veterans Affairs (VA)
1-800-827-1000 (VA Benefits)
1-877-294-6380 (Beneficiaries in receipt of Pension Benefits)
1-877-222-8387 (Health Care Benefits/Income Verification
and Means Testing)
1-800-829-4833 (TDD)
www.va.gov

The VA offers health benefits and services, education assistance, home loans, and burial and memorial benefits to eligible veterans as well as their dependents and survivors. To find a local VA facility, visit the website and click on "Find a VA Facility."

Duff & Phelps
866-282-8258
www.duffandphelps.com

One of the major ratings service companies, Duff & Phelps helps consumers determine the financial strength of an insurance carrier before they purchase a policy.

Eden Alternative
14500 RR 12, Suite 2
Wimberly, TX 78676
512-847-6061

The Eden Alternative is a nonprofit organization dedicated to improving the quality of life for both seniors living in long-term care facilities and those living at home through a variety of means. It is also dedicated to improving the well-being of these seniors' caregivers by celebrating the importance of their work and creating a pleasant and supportive working environment. The organization's work is based on 10 principles, which together focus on creating an "elder-centered community." The Eden Alternative has been widely replicated across the country. Visit the website to view the Eden Alternative Registry.

The Financial Planning Association (FPA)
Suite 400
4100 E. Mississippi Avenue
Denver, CO 80246-3053
1-800-322-4237
www.fpanet.org

The Financial Planning Association has over 100 chapters nationwide that support the organization's more than 28,500 members. On the website, you can read FAQs and tips, learn more about financial planning basics, and find advice and information on tax planning, retirement planning, and estate planning. You can also find a certified financial planner. All members adhere to FPA's strict code of ethics.

Goodwill Industries International
15810 Indianola Drive
Rockville, MD 20855
1-800-741-0186
www.goodwill.org

Goodwill's primary business is to collect donations to sell in its chain of retail stores or online on its website. The organization accepts donations of clothing, jewelry, furniture, household goods, electronics, vehicles, and more. About 85 percent of the revenue generated through these sales funds employment and training programs for people with disabilities and other underserved populations. Donation pick-up is only available in certain communities; call or go online to find out how you can make a tax-deductible donation.

The Green House Project
NCB Capital Impact
2011 Crystal City Drive, Suite 800
Arlington, VA 22202
703-647-2313 (Contact: Marilyn Ellis)
www.thegreenhouseproject.org

The Green House Project builds Green House[rm] homes, which the organization describes as "residences for 6 to 10 elders who require skilled nursing care and want to live a rich life. They are a radical departure from traditional skilled nursing homes and assisted living facilities, altering size, design, and organization to create a warm community." Visit the website and click on "Projects" for a list of Green House projects.

Internal Revenue Service (IRS)
1-800-829-1040
1-800-829-4059 (TDD)

The IRS offers free tax help online, over the phone, and in person. The hours of operation for phone assistance are weekdays from 7:00 A.M. to 10:00 P.M. your local time (Alaska and Hawaii follow PST). On the web, download forms and publications, look up specific tax codes, and learn about tax breaks and new changes in tax laws that may affect you. The IRS also has local offices you may visit to receive in-person assistance. To find an office near you, visit the website and click on "Contact Us" to find your local office.

Meals on Wheels Association of America
203 S. Union Street
Alexandria, VA 22314
703-548-5558
www.mowaa.org

Meals on Wheels is a member organization with senior nutrition programs across the United States that provide nutritious meals to elderly, homebound, disabled, frail, and at-risk individuals. Visit the national website to learn more or locate a program near you.

Medicare Rights Center
1460 Broadway, 11th Floor
New York, NY 10036-7393
1-800-333-4114
www.medicarerights.org

Medicare Rights Center is a nonprofit agency that offers information on Medicare benefits, policies programs, and consumers' rights. The hotline operates from 9:00 A.M. to 3:00 P.M. EST and is staffed by trained counselors who can answer your questions about Medicare.

Moody's
212-553-0300
www.moodys.com

Moody's provides ratings services for the financial industry (among others), helping consumers ascertain the financial strength of an insurance carrier before buying a policy.

National Academy of Elder Law Attorneys (NAELA)
520-881-4005
www.naela.org

NAELA is a nonprofit professional association of attorneys who specialize in elder law. Search their online database to find an elder law attorney near you.

National Adult Protective Services Association (NAPSA)
920 S. Spring Street, Suite 1200
Springfield, IL 62704
217-523-4431
www.apsnetwork.org

A partner in the National Center on Elder Abuse, NAPSA is a national nonprofit member organization comprising adult protective service (APS) programs and concerned individuals in all 50 states, the U.S. Virgin Islands, and Guam. The organization collaborates with and provides support to state and local APS programs through training, research, and outreach. NAPSA's mission is to "improve the quality and availability of protective services for disabled adults and elderly persons who are abused, neglected or exploited and are unable to protect their own interests." Visit the NAPSA site and click on "Report Abuse" for a telephone number to report elder abuse, and for links to the APS program and long-term care ombudsman office in your state.

National Aging in Place Council (NAIPC)
1400 16th Street NW, Suite 420
Washington, DC 20036
202-939-1784
www.naipc.org

Working with individuals and groups from the aging, health care, financial, legal, and design and building sectors, NAIPC focuses on increasing public awareness of and access to home and community-based services that support aging in place. The organization's website features recommended products and offers aging-in-place news and resources, including downloadable booklets on subjects such as home modification and ways to finance aging-in-place initiatives in the home.

National Alliance for Caregiving
301-718-8444
www.caregiving.org

The National Alliance for Caregiving is a nonprofit coalition of national organizations, professional associations, grassroots groups, service organizations, and corporations that serve family caregivers through research, policy analysis, and the development of national programs aimed at increasing public awareness of family caregiving issues. Via its online Family Care Resource Connection, the Alliance rates and reviews books, videos, websites, and other resources of interest to caregivers.

National Association of Area Agencies on Aging (n4a)
1730 Rhode Island Avenue, Suite 1200
Washington, DC 20036
202-872-0888
www.n4a.org

The National Association of Area Agencies on Aging (n4a) is an advocacy organization that supports a national network of 650 Area Agencies on Aging (AAA). The organization champions for services and resources for seniors and people with disabilities. AAAs promote and provide home and community-based services that support aging in place. Call or go online to find your local AAA.

National Association of Home Builders (NAHB)
1201 15th Street, NW
Washington, DC 20005
1-800-368-5242 or 202-266-8200
www.nahb.org

NAHB is a trade association for home builders that offers a wealth of information for consumer homeowners about buying, building, remodeling, and financing a home on its website. NAHB also offers the Certified Aging-in-Place Specialist (CAPS) training program, which covers topics including home modifications for aging in place, common remodeling projects geared toward senior safety, and solutions to common barriers in the home. Specialists with this designation must satisfy ongoing continuing education requirements to stay current. Visit NAHB's website to locate an aging-in-place specialist near you.

National Association of Homecare and Hospice (NAHC)
202-547-7424
www.nahc.org

NAHC is a nonprofit advocacy group that supports aging in place by promoting the availability of health care services in the home. The member body comprises hospices, home care agencies, medical equipment suppliers, and concerned individuals.

National Association of Insurance Commissioners (NAIC)
444 North Capitol Street NW, Suite 701
Washington, DC 20001
202-471-3990
www.naic.org

The National Association of Insurance Commissioners encompasses insurance regulators from all 50 states, the District of Columbia, and the five U.S. territories. Call for your state's department of insurance or go to the website for a direct link. NAIC's website offers free downloadable guides to many different types of insurance, including Medicare Supplemental insurance, long-term care insurance, and home insurance. On the web you can also learn more about individual insurance companies and agents, get rate quotes and comparisons, read insurance buying tips, and file a consumer complaint with your state insurance department.

National Association of Personal Financial Advisors (NAPFA)
3250 North Arlington Heights Road, Suite 109
Arlington Heights, IL 60004
847-483-5400
www.napfa.org

NAPFA is a nonprofit organization that promotes client-centered comprehensive financial planning. Members are fee-only financial advisors. Call for counseling or visit the website to learn more about fee-only financial advising or find a NAPFA-registered financial planner.

National Association of Professional Geriatric Care Managers (NAPGCM)
1604 N. Country Club Road
Tucson, AZ 85716
520-881-8008
www.caremanager.org

NAPGCM is a volunteer nonprofit organization whose mission is "to advance professional geriatric care management through education, collaboration, and leadership." Visit the website to learn more about professional geriatric care managers or locate a care manager from the organization's more than 2,000 members.

National Association of Senior Move Managers (NASMM)
P.O. Box 209
Hinsdale, IL 60522
1-877-606-2766
www.nasmm.com

The National Association of Senior Move Managers is a nonprofit professional association of organizations that help seniors and their families downsize, relocate, and modify their homes. Call or go online to learn more about Senior Move Managers or to find a specialist near you.

National Association of State Veterans Homes
5211 Auth Road
Suitland, MD 20746
301-899-7908
www.nasvh.org

The National Association of State Veterans Homes is a nonprofit organization whose membership is composed of administrators and staff from veterans homes across the country. The association has a dual mission: to ensure that all veterans receive the benefits, services, and care that they are eligible for; and to ensure that the level of care and services in veterans homes meets the highest standards of quality. Visit the website for a directory of state homes.

National Center for Independent Living (CIL)
710 Rhode Island Avenue Northwest, 5th Floor
Washington, DC 20036
1-877-525-3400
202-207-0340 (TTY)

NCIL is a membership organization that promotes independent living and advocates for the rights of people with disabilities. Visit the website to find a Center for Independent Living or Statewide Independent Living Council near you.

National Center on Elder Abuse (NCEA)
c/o Center for Community Research and Services
University of Delaware
297 Graham Hall
Newark, DE 19716
302-831-3525
www.ncea.aoa.gov

Directed by the U.S. Administration on Aging, the NCEA is a national resource center committed to collaborating with and supporting national, state, and local partners as they help older Americans live with dignity and independence, and free from abuse, neglect, and exploitation. The NCEA educates professionals and the public about elder abuse, provides training and assistance to states and community-based organizations, aids in program and policy development, and more. The organization also maintains a state resource directory on its website where you can find help lines, hotlines, and other resources; as well as information on state government agencies, and state-specific laws, regulations, and statistics.

National Citizens' Coalition for Nursing Home Reform (NCCNHR)
202-332-2276
1828 L Street, NW, Suite 801
Washington, DC 20036
202-332-2276
www.nccnhr.org

The National Citizens' Coalition for Nursing Home Reform is a nonprofit grassroots organization that lobbies at the state and federal levels for fundamental improvements in nursing homes with regard to issues ranging from residents' rights to increased wages and benefits for staff members, and it works to bring public attention to substandard conditions. The Coalition works with nursing home employees' unions, ombudsman agencies, residents and their families, and other concerned groups and individuals to enact change. NCCNHR's website is a one-stop shop for locating your state ombudsman, learning about residents' rights and government policies regarding nursing homes, downloading fact sheets and publications, and more.

National Council of Independent Living (NCIL)
1916 Wilson Boulevard, Suite 209
Arlington, VA 22201
703-525-3406
703-525-4153 (TTY)
www.ncil.org

NCIL is a membership organization run by and for people with disabilities, which promotes independent living and advocates for the rights of disabled people. The organization makes referrals to independent living communities, and provides consumer support and information on its website. Centers for Independent Living (CILs) and Statewide Independent Living Councils (SILCs) are programs of NCIL.

National Council on the Aging (NCOA)
300 D Street SW, Suite 801
Washington, DC 20024
202-479-1200
www.ncoa.org

NCOA is a nonprofit service and advocacy organization that focuses on the issues of older adults. The organization works with other nonprofits, businesses, and government "to help seniors live independently, find jobs and benefits, improve their health, and remain active in their communities." NCOA also offers Benefits CheckUp, an online tool that helps seniors who have limited income and resources to connect with benefit programs that help with routine expenses including prescription drug costs, food, rent, and energy bills. See Appendix B for more information on Benefits CheckUp.

National Guardianship Association (NGA)
174 Crestview Drive
Bellefonte, PA 16823
1-877-326-5992
www.guardianship.org

The NGA is a member organization of guardianship practitioners, allied professionals, and family guardians. The association provides information and resources for guardianship on its website, where you can also find a professional guardian in your area.

National Hospice and Palliative Care Organization (NHPCO)
1731 King Street, Suite 100
Alexandria, VA 22314
703-837-1500 (Main Line)
1-800-658-8898 (Helpline)
1-877-658-8896 (Multilingual Helpline)
www.nhpco.org

NHPCO is the largest nonprofit member organization of hospice and palliative care programs and professionals in the United States. NHPCO advocates for the terminally ill and their families in a number of ways. Call the helpline for free information on hospice care and for information about your local hospice programs.

National Long Term Care Ombudsmen Resource Center
1828 L Street NW, Suite 801
Washington, DC 20036
202-332-2275
www.ltcombudsman.org

Funded by the AoA and run by the NCCNHR, the National Long Term Care Ombudsman Resource Center provides training and support to the 53 state long-term care ombudsman programs. Call or go online to find your state ombudsman.

National Network of Estate Planning Attorneys
1-800-638-8681
www.netplanning.com

The National Network of Estate Planning Attorneys is a member organization of attorneys who specialize in estate planning. Visit the website to learn more about estate plans and the process of estate planning, and to locate an attorney in your area.

National PACE Association (NPA)
801 N. Fairfax Street, Suite 309
Alexandria, VA 22314
703-535-1565
www.npaonline.org

The National PACE Association is a member organization of Programs of All-Inclusive Care for the Elderly (PACE). The association supports local PACE programs in a variety of ways, particularly through education and research. You can find out more about PACE programs and get information on federal and state policies by visiting NPA's website.

Rehabilitation Engineering and Assistive Technology Society of North
America (RESNA)
703-524-6686
www.resna.org

RESNA is a nonprofit organization that promotes the advancement of assistive technology through research and development, education, and advocacy.

Salvation Army National Headquarters
615 Slaters Lane
P.O. Box 269
Alexandria, VA 22313
1-800-SA-TRUCK (1-800-728-7825)
www.salvationarmyusa.org

The Salvation Army is a national charitable organization that offers a variety
of community-based programs to help people in need. The Salvation Army
accepts donations of clothing, furniture, assorted household goods, sporting equipment, books, electronics, and more. You can make a tax-deductible
donation and schedule a pickup by calling the toll-free number above. The
organization also sponsors a number of programs for elderly adults, which
include activities programs, community centers, senior camping, residential
facilities, and adult day care services. Visit the website for more information
on programs available in your area.

Seniors Real Estate Specialists (SRES) Council
430 N. Michigan Avenue
Chicago, IL 60611
1-800-500-4564
www.seniorsrealestate.com

The SRES council offers its namesake Seniors Real Estate Specialist Designation Course to Realtors who specialize in, or plan to specialize in, the
senior housing market. The course covers topics such as senior-specific
housing options (i.e., age-restricted housing); aging-in-place design; reverse
mortgages; using a variety of income sources such as pensions, 401Ks, and
IRAs in real estate transactions; and working with other senior specialists
such as estate planners and reverse mortgage lenders. To become a designee,

students must complete the course and score 80 percent or higher on the exam, and also maintain membership with the National Association of REALTORS®. Visit the SRES website to locate a specialist near you.

Social Security Administration (SSA)
1-800-772-1213
1-800-325-0778 (TTY)
www.socialsecurity.gov

The Social Security Administration is the agency of the U.S. federal government that administers social security benefits. On the website, you can apply for benefits, locate your local Social Security office, request important documents, and even estimate your benefits. See Appendix B for more information on estimating benefits.

Society of Financial Service Professionals
17 Campus Boulevard, Suite 201
Newtown Square, PA 19073-3230
610-526-2500
www.financialpro.org

The Society of Financial Service Professionals is the longest-established professional organization for financial service professionals in the United States. With a membership base of almost 18,000 members, you can find expert assistance on topics ranging from estate, retirement, and financial planning to life, health, disability, and long-term care insurance.

Standard & Poor's
55 Water Street
New York, NY 10041
212-438-2000
www.standardandpoors.com

Standard & Poor's provides ratings for insurance carries so you can determine the financial strength of the company before purchasing a policy.

State Health Insurance Assistance Programs (SHIP)
1-800-633-4227

There are SHIPs in every state that offer free counseling and advice on Medicare insurance plans and your Medicare rights. Call or go to www. medicare.gov (search for "SHIP") to find the phone number for the program in your state.

State Medical Assistance Office (Medicaid)
1-800-MEDICARE
1-877-486-2048 (TTY)
www.medicare.gov

Medicaid and Medicare offices can provide information on programs that help pay for nursing home costs as well as community services for low-income seniors. To find the State Medical Assistance Office in your state, visit www.medicare.gov and click on "Find Helpful Phone Numbers and Websites" or call the numbers listed above.

U.S. Department of Veterans Affairs (VA)
810 Vermont Avenue, NW
Washington, DC 20420
1-800-827-1000
www.va.gov

Formerly known as the Veterans Administration, the Department of Veterans Affairs administers veterans' benefits programs for veterans, survivors, and eligible family members. Contact for complete information on veterans' benefits.

Visiting Nurse Association of America (VNA)
900 19th Street, NW, Suite 200
Washington, DC 20006
202-384-1420
www.vnaa.org

VNAA's membership comprises Visiting Nurse Agencies (VNAs) and home health care providers across the United States. The organization's goal is to make visiting nurse services and home health care widely available and affordable, particularly for elderly and disabled individuals. Visit the website to locate a VNA near you.

Weiss Ratings
15430 Endeavor Drive
Jupiter, FL 33478
561-354-4400
www.weissratings.com

Weiss Ratings is one of the major ratings services, providing ratings of insurance companies in order to help consumers determine the financial strength and solvency of the company before they purchase a policy.

Worksheets and Checklists

Plan early. Be prepared. Those are two of the guiding principles of this book. Of course, it's not always possible to be prepared for everything—you can't prepare for a sudden and unexpected change in health, or an accident. But you can plan ahead, and if you do so, you will be ahead of the curve if something happens that is beyond your control.

Use the worksheets and checklists in this appendix to guide you as you look ahead at your choices for senior housing and senior care, and to record important information about your finances, insurance coverage, attorney and legal considerations, doctors and specialists, emergency contact person, medications, home health and home care needs, monthly income and expenses, moving day needs, and storage facility. Having all of this information recorded in one place will help you and your family ensure that all of your affairs are in order as you make these critical decisions. And remember to always keep sensitive information in a safe place.

Financial Information

If you have designated a power of attorney to make financial decisions on your behalf once you are unable to do so, make a copy of this worksheet once you have filled it out and give it to that person. Keep a copy for your records.

Social Security

Social Security number: _____

Bank Accounts

Name of bank: _____

Bank address: _____

_____

Bank phone number: _____

Account type (e.g., checking, savings): _____

Account number: _____

Name(s) on account: _____

Name of bank: _____

Bank address: _____

_____

Bank phone number: _____

Account type (e.g., checking, savings): _____

Account number: _____

Name(s) on account: _____

Investments

Type of investment: _____

Location of investment: _____

How can it be accessed? _____

_____

Type of investment: _____

Location of investment: _____

How can it be accessed? _____

_____

Type of investment: _____

Location of investment: _____

How can it be accessed? _____

_____

Safety Deposit Box

Name of bank: _____

Bank address: _____

_____

Where is the key? _____

Who can sign? _____

Trust

Established by: _____

Established for: _____

Name of attorney: _____

Attorney's phone number: _____

Location of trust: _____

People with copies of trust papers: _____

_____

Phone numbers for those people: _____

_____

Financial Advisor

Name of advisor: _____

Name of firm: _____

Address: _____

_____

Phone number: _____

E-mail address: _____

Notes

Insurance Information

If you have designated a power of attorney to make health care decisions on your behalf once you are unable to do so, make a copy of this worksheet once you have filled it out and give it to that person. Keep a copy for your records.

Primary Medical Insurance

Type of insurance: _____

Name of insurer: _____

Policy number: _____

Phone number: _____

Supplemental Medical Insurance

Type of insurance: _____

Name of insurer: _____

Policy number: _____

Phone number: _____

Medicare Part D

Name of insurer: _____

Policy number: _____

Phone number: _____

Long-Term Care Insurance

Name of insurer: _____

Policy number: _____

Phone number: _____

Name of agent: _____

What is the coverage and terms (where and how long will it pay benefits)?

_____

_____

How long is the waiting period?   _____

How many deficiencies are required before the policy can be activated?

_____

_____

Life Insurance

Name of insurer: _____

Policy number: _____

Location of policy: _____

Beneficiary: _____

Phone number: _____

Funeral Policy

Location of policy: _____

Name of funeral home: _____

Location of funeral home: _____

_____

Funeral home phone number: _____

What does the policy cover?   _____

_____

Notes

_____

_____

Legal Information and Documents

Keep hard copies of your powers of attorney documents on hand at home in case they need to be accessed in the event of an emergency. If you have an attorney, make a copy of this worksheet once you have filled it out and give it to your attorney. Keep a copy for your records.

Attorney

Name of attorney: _____

Name of law firm: _____

Address: _____

_____

Phone number: _____

E-mail address: _____

Will

Name of attorney: _____

Attorney's phone number: _____

Location of original papers: _____

People with original copies of the will: _____

_____

Phone numbers for those people: _____

_____

Guardianship

Location of document: _____

Name of guardian: _____

Phone number: _____

E-mail address: _____

Power of Attorney (financial)

Name of primary agent: _____

Phone number for primary agent: _____

E-mail address: _____

Name of secondary agent: _____

Phone number for secondary agent: _____

E-mail address: _____

Name of attorney: _____

Phone number for attorney: _____

Location of original document: _____

Names of people with copies: _____

_____

Phone numbers for those people: _____

_____

Power of Attorney (health care/medical)

Name of primary agent: _____

Phone number for primary agent: _____

E-mail address: _____

Name of secondary agent: _____

Phone number for secondary agent: _____

E-mail address: _____

Name of attorney: _____

Phone number for attorney: _____

Location of original document: _____

Names of people with copies: _____

_____

Phone numbers for those people: _____

_____

Living Will (a.k.a. directive to physicians)

Location of document: _____

Names of people with copies: _____

Phone numbers for those people: _____

_____

Do Not Resuscitate (DNR) Order

Is there a DNR on medical record (Y/N)? _____

Notes

_____

_____

_____

_____

_____

_____

_____

_____

_____

_____

_____

_____

_____

Doctors, Other Health Care Specialists, and Emergency Contact Information

Keep this worksheet updated and make copies to leave with each of your health care specialists and your emergency contact person. Keep a hard copy on hand at home.

Primary Care Physician

Name of doctor: _____

Address: _____

_____

Phone number: _____

E-mail address: _____

Is there a DNR on medical record (Y/N)? _____

Date of last visit: _____

Notes

_____

_____

_____

_____

_____

_____

_____

_____

_____

_____

_____

Geriatric Care Manager (GCM)

Name of GCM: _____

Address: _____

_____

Phone number: _____

E-mail address: _____

Is there a care/service plan in place (Y/N)? _____

Date of last assessment: _____

Notes

_____

_____

_____

_____

_____

_____

_____

_____

_____

_____

_____

_____

_____

_____

_____

_____

Home Care/Home Health Care

Name of caregiver(s): _____

_____

Is the caregiver an agency worker or independent contractor?

_____

Agency name: _____

Address: _____

_____

Phone number (business hours): _____

Phone number (after business hours): _____

Contact person: _____

Caregiver visiting schedule: _____

_____

Is there a care/service plan in place (Y/N)? _____

Date of last assessment: _____

Notes

_____

_____

_____

_____

_____

_____

_____

_____

_____

_____

Specialist

Name of specialist: _____

Address: _____

_____

Phone number: _____

E-mail address: _____

Date of last visit: _____

Notes

_____

_____

_____

_____

_____

_____

_____

_____

_____

_____

_____

_____

_____

_____

_____

_____

_____

_____

_____

Specialist

Name of specialist: _____

Address: _____

_____

Phone number: _____

E-mail address: _____

Date of last visit: _____

Notes

_____

_____

_____

_____

_____

_____

_____

_____

_____

_____

_____

_____

_____

_____

_____

_____

_____

_____

Specialist

Address: _____

_____

Phone number: _____

E-mail address: _____

Date of last visit: _____

Notes

_____

_____

_____

_____

_____

_____

_____

_____

_____

_____

_____

_____

_____

_____

_____

_____

_____

_____

Emergency Contact Person

Name of contact: _____

Address: _____

_____

Phone number: _____

E-mail address: _____

Relationship: _____

Notes

_____

_____

_____

_____

_____

_____

_____

_____

_____

_____

_____

_____

_____

_____

_____

_____

_____

_____

Medications Tracker

List all medications you are currently taking and drugs you have stopped taking within the last six months. Medications can stay in your system long after you stop taking them. Make a copy to give to your primary care physician so he is aware of all the medications you are taking, and those you have stopped taking recently. This will help him prevent contraindications from occurring. Keep a hard copy on hand at home.

If you need more space to list medications, make a copy of this list before filling it in.

Medication: _____

Dosage (how much and how often?): _____

_____

Date prescribed: _____

Start date: _____

End date (if applicable): _____

Name of prescribing doctor: _____

Phone number of doctor: _____

Reason for medication: _____

Have you experienced any side effects* (Y/N)? _____

If yes, explain: _____

_____

Aid or monitoring required? _____

Medication: _____

Dosage (how much and how often?): _____

_____

Date prescribed: _____

Start date: _____

End date (if applicable): _____

Name of prescribing doctor: _____

Phone number of doctor: _____

Reason for medication: _____

Have you experienced any side effects* (Y/N)? _____

If yes, explain: _____

_____

Aid or monitoring required? _____

Medication: _____

Dosage (how much and how often?): _____

_____

Date prescribed: _____

Start date: _____

End date (if applicable): _____

Name of prescribing doctor: _____

Phone number of doctor: _____

Reason for medication: _____

Have you experienced any side effects* (Y/N)? _____

If yes, explain: _____

_____

Aid or monitoring required? _____

Medication: _____

Dosage (how much and how often?): _____

_____

Date prescribed: _____

Start date: _____

End date (if applicable): _____

Name of prescribing doctor: _____

Phone number of doctor: _____

Reason for medication: _____

Have you experienced any side effects* (Y/N)? _____

If yes, explain: _____

_____

Aid or monitoring required? _____

Medication: _____

Dosage (how much and how often?): _____

_____

Date prescribed: _____

Start date: _____

End date (if applicable): _____

Name of prescribing doctor: _____

Phone number of doctor: _____

Reason for medication: _____

Have you experienced any side effects* (Y/N)? _____

If yes, explain: _____

_____

Aid or monitoring required? _____

Notes

_____

_____

_____

_____

_____

_____

_____

_____

_____

_____

_____

_____

_____

_____

_____

_____

_____

_____

*If you have experienced any side effects from the medications you are taking, write them down, including details about what time they occurred, how long they lasted, how severe they were, and whether they occur regularly. This information can help your doctor determine whether your medications are safe and effective for your condition.

Home Care and Home Health: Determining Your Needs

Before you start home care or home health care, think about these two questions: What do you need? And what do you want? Receiving care in your home is very personal. No matter where or how you find your caregiver, ultimately you will have the most success in finding a caregiver whose skills, experience, and personal manner are most suited to you if you are able to identify your needs and preferences and communicate them clearly before you start working together. Use the following checklist to help you establish your needs and preferences, then communicate them to your caregiver, or the agency you choose to place a caregiver in your home.

☐ Do you need home care (custodial) or home health care (skilled)?

_____

☐ If you require home health care, do you have a doctor's prescription?

☐ What kinds of things do you need assistance with? Check all that apply:

  ☐ Bathing

  ☐ Dressing

  ☐ Grooming

  ☐ Using the toilet

  ☐ Eating assistance

  ☐ Light housekeeping

  ☐ Medication reminders

  ☐ Medication administration

  ☐ Physical, occupational, or speech therapy

  ☐ Walking

  ☐ Transferring (e.g., from bed to wheelchair)

  ☐ Other _____

  ☐ Other _____

☐ Do you prefer a nonsmoking caregiver?

☐ Do you prefer a male or female caregiver? _____

☐ When and how often do you need a caregiver? Do you anticipate that it will change in the near future?

_____

☐ What duties do you need the caregiver to perform, and how often (e.g., helping with grooming each morning, and bathing every other day)?

_____

_____

☐ Do you need incontinence care or another type of specialized care?

_____

☐ Do you have any religious or cultural habits or traditions that your caregiver should know about so she can accommodate them?

_____

☐ Do you have any food preferences, sensitivities, or allergies?

_____

☐ Would you prefer a bilingual caregiver? _____

☐ Do you have any pet peeves that your caregiver should know about (e.g., messiness, tardiness, or smoking)?

_____

Notes

_____

_____

_____

_____

_____

_____

Home Care and Home Health: Interviewing an Agency

The home care or home health care agency you choose will help you establish a schedule and determine how many hours and/or visits are appropriate for your needs. Use the following checklist as a guide, and insert your own questions as they arise.

General Practices

- Will a licensed nurse perform my initial assessment? What does the assessment entail?

- How often will I be reassessed? How often will my care plan be reevaluated? (Every 30 days or as needed is best.)

- Will the intake nurse review my medications during my assessment?

- Can you have someone evaluate my home for safety and provide additional home safety and/or medical tips for in-home care?

- Can visits be tailored according to the schedule I specify?

- Are caregivers able to take my blood pressure?

- Do you provide both temporary and long-term assistance?

- If I need long-term assistance and will be paying out of pocket, do you offer a discounted rate?

- What if I need different tasks done on each visit?

- Can I request a nonsmoking caregiver?

- Will my caregiver call before arriving?

- What should I do if my caregiver is late or leaves early?

- Other: _____

Management

- Do you provide ongoing supervision of your caregivers? How often do check-ins occur? (Weekly or as needed is ideal.)

- Do you require progress reports? How regularly?

- Do you cover all payroll taxes for your caregivers?

- Are caregivers available 24 hours a day?

- Are supervisors on call 24 hours a day?

- If I request a new caregiver, how long will it take to send a replacement? (More than 48 hours is unreasonable.)

- How long will it take to cover a shift if my caregiver calls in sick?

- If my caregiver is sick, will she call me directly? How will I know if a replacement caregiver is on the way?

- Will I be guaranteed the same caregiver every time? Can I request it?

- Can I make requests to my caregiver for how I want things to be done, or do I call the agency to specify this?

- Other: _____

Services

- Do you provide medication management (ordering medications, assembling pillboxes, providing verbal medication reminders)?

- Can caregivers provide bathing assistance?

- Do caregivers provide transportation for errands and doctor's appointments?

- Are caregivers able to assist in transfers (lifting me from bed or bath to wheelchair)?

- Can caregivers provide wound care (especially for surgery or bed sores)?

- Is cooking assistance available?

- Is light housekeeping assistance available? What kind of tasks can I request (e.g., laundry, tidying up)?

- Do you provide vital signs monitoring and diabetic monitoring?

- Are your caregivers experienced with stroke or surgery recovery exercises?

- Do you offer physical, occupational, and speech therapy?

- Can you do shopping and run errands for me?

- Can my caregiver help me with walking and assist me with a cane or walker?

- Is the nurse available by phone if I have questions regarding my care?

- Other: _____

Insurance Coverage

- Do you have professional liability coverage?

- Do you provide worker's compensation insurance?

- If my caregiver drives me to an appointment or takes me out for an errand, is it covered by insurance?

- Are your caregivers bonded and insured?

- Are your caregivers required to renew their state licenses?

- Do you conduct background checks on all staff? What is involved?

- What kind of insurance do you accept? Will you get pre-authorization and bill my insurance company directly?

- Other: _____

Qualifications and Training

- What are the qualifications of the owners?

- What are the qualifications of the person who will do my initial assessment?

- What are the qualifications of the person who will be my caregiver?

- Are all caregivers trained in CPR and first aid? Are their certifications current?

- How long has the caregiver you will match me with been employed with your company?

- What areas of ongoing training do you provide your staff? How often do you offer this training?

- Other: _____

Availability and Scheduling

- How soon could you send a caregiver?

- Is assistance available on weekends?

- How often can I schedule visits?

- How long are caregiver visits?

- How can I reach the agency after regular business hours?

- Is there someone I can call in case of emergency?

- Other: _____

Costs

- Is there an initial registration fee?

- Do you charge for the initial assessment? Is there a reassessment fee?

- Are there any other upfront fees or administrative costs?

- What is the hourly rate?

- Do you charge mileage for transportation or running errands? What is the rate?

- Do you charge for travel time and/or mileage to and from my home?

- Other: _____

Notes

_____

_____

_____

_____

_____

_____

_____

_____

_____

Monthly Income and Expenses

Fill in the amounts for your monthly income and expenses in the following tables. What is the difference between your total monthly income and total monthly expenses? That amount is the money that you will have left over for incidentals. Do you have enough left over each month to live comfortably? If not, book an appointment with a financial advisor and bring this worksheet with you to your first meeting.

Income	Amount
Retirement	$_____
Pension	$_____
Social Security	$_____
Investment(s)	$_____
Other income	$_____
Total	**$_____**

Expenses	Amount
Mortgage payment/rent	$_____
Car loan	$_____
Utility bills	$_____
Groceries	$_____
Prescription medications	$_____
Medical co-pays	$_____
Insurance premiums	$_____
Other expenses	$_____
Total	**$_____**

Notes

_____

_____

_____

Moving Day

Moving day is hectic, no matter where you're coming from or where you're going. The following checklists will help keep you organized from the start. First, remember to breathe! When you get to your new home, focus on one room at a time when you unpack, and don't exhaust or hurt yourself. Don't spend all night unpacking, either. It's better to get a good night's sleep and resume the job in the morning. Arrange for your family to call once or twice a day for the first few days after you move in. They can bring things that you have forgotten, or simply provide reassurance during this period of transition.

Tips for Getting Started

- ☐ Create a floor that details the rooms in the new residence. Post it on the front door of the new residence so movers know where to put the boxes.

- ☐ Replicate the old environment if you can. Photograph your closet, your china cabinet, medicine cabinet, etc. Your loved ones can help set things up in your new home so that they are as familiar as possible, easing your period of adjustment.

Logistics

- ☐ Confirm that you have transportation to the facility.

- ☐ Confirm that family and friends are meeting you at the facility, and that you are meeting at a specified time.

Safety

- ☐ Coordinate with your contact person if you will need a wheelchair or other assistance with your move.

- ☐ Make sure the elevator is in order.

Unpacking

- ☐ Set up the bedroom first. Make it comfortable (e.g., make the bed, clear away clutter, and set up lamps).

- ☐ Unpack your clothing and toiletries.

- [ ] Unpack the kitchen and living areas after the bedroom.
- [ ] Check to make sure the grab bars near the bed and in the bathroom are secure.
- [ ] Make sure you know how to operate the call system, telephone, TV, thermostat, stove, microwave, sink, shower, door locks, elevator radio, etc. If you don't know how, ask a staff member for assistance.

Staff and Residents

- [ ] Introduce yourself to staff members you haven't met yet.
- [ ] If you have a question or problem, make sure you know who you should go to.

Miscellaneous

- [ ] Are you comfortable? Do you know where everything is?
- [ ] Do you have everything you need (e.g., toiletries, incontinence supplies)?
- [ ] Confirm upcoming appointments and transportation with staff.

Notes

_____

_____

_____

_____

_____

_____

_____

_____

_____

_____

_____

Storage Facility

If you have any items in storage, fill out the following worksheet so that your family can locate and access your belongings if necessary.

Storage

Name of storage facility: _____

Address: _____

_____

Phone number: _____

Account number: _____

Name(s) on account: _____

Where is the inventory of items? _____

Are items insured (Y/N)? _____

Name of insurer (if not insured by facility): _____

_____

Phone number of insurer: _____

How can the storage unit be accessed? _____

_____

Where is the key? _____

Notes

_____

_____

_____

_____

_____

_____

Index

H

I

Q–R